Given

by the

Lincoln Christian College

Alumni Association

As Part

of a

$100,000 Gift,

1968-1971

FAITH
TAKES A NAME

FAITH
TAKES A NAME

By DWIGHT E. STEVENSON

HARPER & BROTHERS
PUBLISHERS
NEW YORK

Contents

43619

Contents

Acknowledgments

This book will be going to press while the author is on the high seas, bound for a "sabbatical year" in the Philippines. The absence of the author at such a critical time has put an undue burden upon the editor, John B. Chambers, and a number of others, especially Roscoe M. Pierson, Librarian of The College of the Bible, who has assumed many of the duties which normally would have been carried by the writer. Proofreading, copyright permissions, decisions about format, jacket design—all have fallen upon these friends.

Thanks are due to Dolores Von Nostrand and Marilyn Taylor, faculty secretaries at The College of the Bible, who have acted as typists.

We are glad to acknowledge here the courtesy of the following persons and publishers who have graciously permitted us to quote from their copyrighted works: Burns, Oates & Washbourne, Ltd. for "In No Strange Land" by Francis Thompson; Christian Board of Publication for the selections from the author's *Faiths that Compete for My Loyalty* and *Strong Son of God*; the

7

Division of Christian Education of the National Council of the Churches of Christ in the United States of America for selections from *The Holy Bible: American Standard Version* and *Revised Standard Version*; Hermann Hagedorn for "The Bomb That Fell on America"; Harcourt, Brace and Company for the selection from *The Rock* by T. S. Eliot and for "Four Preludes on Playthings" from *Smoke and Steel* by Carl Sandburg; Virgil Markham for "Outwitted" from *Poems of Edwin Markham*, selected and arranged by Charles L. Wallis; Charles Scribner's Sons for "What Are We?" from *A Stone, A Leaf, A Door* selected by John S. Barnes; University of Chicago Press for selections from *The Apocrypha, An American Translation* by Edgar J. Goodspeed.

DWIGHT E. STEVENSON

Introduction

Christianity for at least a decade after Pentecost was a faith in quest of a name. With many today it is a name in quest of a faith.

In the beginning the sense of the Holy Spirit was great upon the believers. It baptized the disciples with power, multiplied their number, bound them into a vital fellowship, brought them into conflict with their fellow Jews, dispersed them in persecution, spread their faith like a contagion.

The Spirit had come! But it brought no blueprints. The new movement had no name, no buildings, no organization, no scriptures of its own, and no liturgy. These grew out of the living Word through the testing of the years. This is to say that the disciples were not like generals plotting a campaign over a familiar field; rather, they were like explorers opening a new continent. They had no map, but the lure of new lands was strong within them. And as they advanced, Christianity took on definition; they came step by step to possess "a habitation and a name."

Among the most revealing landmarks which the new faith left in the wake of its progress were the early names by which these "believers" called themselves—*disciples, brethren, believers, saints, those of the way, the fellowship*. There were others. These names are more than designations; they are descriptions. When taken together they give a rich content to the one name which finally arose to include them all and to supersede them—the name *Christians*. We can learn much about being Christians from a study of these names. This is what we now propose: a kind of backtracking on the trail of our faith, from its name to its ways as these ways are shown in some of the New Testament synonyms of *Christians*.

The need for such a movement from name to faith is apparent. We are Christians—and not in name only. In a real sense, the Christian faith is deeply rooted in us. We cannot remember having reasoned our way into it, or recall having decided for it in preference to some rival faith. In most of us, it exists below the level of thought and speech as a formless body of internal values, vaguely felt. Therefore it would be proper to say that the faith is in us, but we are not fully in the faith.

The reason for this predicament lies in the fact that we *inherited* our Christianity from a long line of spiritual ancestors. Consequently, the faith itself comes to us closely intertwined with its secondary products—with church buildings, clerical orders, creedal statements, and accepted social customs. It also comes to us intertwined with American democracy and with the values of Western civilization—humanitarianism, science, progress, technology. Moreover, we are at the receiving end of its power in history, rather than at its generating source. Others have labored and we have reaped the fruits of their toil. Others have been martyred and we, without much thought or gratitude, have accepted the boons guaranteed by their sacrifices. In the light of these facts, it becomes clear that what passes for Christianity among us is often little more than conformity or respectability. Frequently it is a confused, half-paganized self-righteousness.

Such an indeterminate faith seems satisfying to few who hold it. It brings neither consolation nor courage. What is more, it is inadequate as a social force. It empowers us neither to endure the shipwreck of an old world nor to lay the keel of a new one. And it does not brace us for the current clash with Christianity's most ardent and ruthless foe since Islam threatened to overrun Europe in the seventh and eighth centuries.

In the pages that follow we shall not be interested in "the Christian faith" as a formulation of creedal principles for the contemplation of armchair minds. We shall try to see it as it was when it began—as a way of life offering salvation to those living in darkness and in the shadow of death. This faith is a militant way. Its conflicts with paganism are genuine engagements. Its victories and defeats are the stuff of human destiny. For it is our conviction that Christianity is not only an "alternative to Communism"; it is an alternative to Western civilization as well—the means of purging and transfiguring it for the new chapter of planetary man just beginning.

The method of this book is simply that of studying twelve New Testament synonyms for the word *Christian*. Many of these names are a decade older than the name *Christian* itself. A glance at them reveals facets of meaning which the earliest believers found in their faith, and which we may recover in ours. It is our expectation that anyone who makes the study will emerge from it, not only a more intelligent Christian, but also a more committed one.

The book deals with only twelve synonyms—those making up the chapter headings. It is the author's belief that these are the important ones, and that most of the meanings of other terms that might have been studied have been gathered into these twelve. It will be noticed that these terms all appear as plurals. That is the form they take in the New Testament. The fact is suggestive: the individual, isolated Christian is an anomaly. If he is truly a Christian he never stands alone, but he always seeks his brother, and his Lord.

FAITH
TAKES A NAME

I ⋇ Disciples

And the word of God increased; and the number of the disciples multiplied greatly. . . . ACTS 6:7[1]

If you continue in my word, you are truly my disciples. . . .
JOHN 8:31

So Barnabas went to Tarsus to look for Saul; and when he had found him, he brought him to Antioch. For a whole year they met with the church, and taught a large company of people; and in Antioch the disciples were for the first time called Christians.
ACTS 11:25, 26

IF THE disciples were called *Christians* for the first time at Antioch, as Luke tells us, then Christians called themselves *disciples* for at least a dozen years before the name *Christian* was invented. The earlier term, while not an exclusive title during these first years, must have been a favorite one. In the book of Acts it appears no less

[1] Unless otherwise indicated, Scriptural quotations are from *The Holy Bible: American Standard Version,* copyright, 1901, by Thomas Nelson & Sons, 1929, by the Division of Christian Education of the National Council of the Churches of Christ in the U.S.A.; *The Holy Bible: Revised Standard Version,* copyright, 1946, 1952, by the Division of Christian Education of the National Council of the Churches of Christ in the U.S.A.

15

than thirty times. Why the term was popular is not difficult to see. It identified the members of the early church
with the Twelve and with the other disciples who had
accompanied Jesus from the baptism to the resurrection.
Thus considered, the whole body of believers was simply
an enlargement of the Galilean company that had attached itself to the Great Teacher during his ministry.
The name tied them in closest intimacy to the historical
Jesus and infused into them the consecrated spirit of the
first followers.

The appeal of the early name was not confined to the
primitive church. Leaping the centuries, it has fastened
itself upon the religious communion, the Disciples of
Christ; and it is frequently used in its original, unde-
nominational sense throughout modern Christendom.
Well it might be. Older than any title for the faithful,
the name *disciple* throws revealing light on the meaning
of our Christian profession. If we are Christians, we are
disciples. What, then, are disciples?

If we are disciples, we are personally attached to Jesus.
This is what discipleship meant in the beginning. Forsaking old vocations, severing long-established loyalties,
and quitting familiar scenes, the first disciples cast in
their lot with the Nazarene with complete abandon. They
attached themselves to him and followed him with confidence. Their attachment was personal—not to his commands, nor even to his principles—but to him.

In the religion of the Christian, Jesus himself occupies a larger place than any of his teachings or any doctrine about him. Loyalty is stronger than orthodoxy, richer, and more alive. Communion of Teacher and friend comes before conviction. The relationship of "me and Thee" is more precious than the more egoistic and impersonal "I and it," even when "it" stands for truth; for in the Christian sense no ultimate truth is merely something known. Truth is life, and life is love. In a genuinely personal attachment, we cleave to the core of reality.

This insight of the personal quality in Christian faith is fugitive. It keeps eluding us. Perhaps a modern example will enable us to see it more clearly. Forearmed by a premonition of danger to Gandhi, Vincent Sheean had traveled halfway around the world, all the way from his Vermont farm to Delhi, just to be near the Mahatma in his hour of need. When the martyrdom came, Sheean was present, and in that moment he received from the Indian leader an impression so deep that, even with Gandhi gone, he continues to live under its spell. *Lead, Kindly Light,* the book that records these experiences, is more than a tribute; it is a declaration of faith. "Gandhi himself, by his words, acts and death, had . . . set up such a tremendous earthquake in my own being that I was compelled, from now on and henceforth, to accept his central truth as being not only his view, but, by compelling evidence imposed upon me after his death, the simple truth as it is and ever will be." If Gandhi set up such an earthquake in the soul of an American journalist, what kind of spiritual tremors must Jesus have released in the lives of his disciples? They, and all who are drawn into their company, felt called and compelled. Through him as a person they looked deep into the heart of cosmic truth.

Jesus as a person captivates us. In him we find "the highest and holiest manhood," revealing to each of us the depths lying undeveloped within. In him God breaks through upon human life. Formerly men had no trouble believing in the power of God; the forces of nature were evidence enough of that. They had difficulty believing in his goodness. Since Jesus came they have found a convincing reassurance that God is good.

What Jesus was and did still remains the best piece of good news the human race has ever heard. A life ruled absolutely by love! What strength do we whose love is so sporadic and broken-winged take from that. A life with no shadow of selfishness! How our darkened, selfish souls are illumined by it. A life complete in its sympathy for others! How our wounds are healed by it. A life that knew defeat, drinking the cup of woe to its dregs, but found that God keeps watch above his own. How that lifts us from despair.

The charm of that life! Jesus drew men, and he held

them. He fired them with a lifelong passion. The reach
of that life! He is "our eternal contemporary." The
radiance of that life! He is humanity in its completeness
and divinity in its fulfillment. The power of that life!
He draws all men to himself.

With Jesus, the divine life stopped being a speculation,
a dream, an ideal, and began to be a fact in human history.
That God does not remain aloof in his far heaven, but
that he is here among men, bearing our burdens, feeling
our pain, carrying our sorrows, struggling with us in the
upward moral pull—here is the good news that comes
into the world through Jesus.

The attachment of discipleship is to Jesus as a person
who incarnates truth, and it sets up a personal relation
which becomes a growing experience of truth as love.
This attachment is costly.

Jesus himself bade his followers consider the cost. Let
no one, he said, be like a king with puny forces declaring
war against a formidable military power; or like a con-
tractor who could get together the labor and materials for
nothing more than the foundation of a tower. Such
foundation stones, crumbling in the weather and bleach-
ing in the sun, lie useless in the busy city of men silently
mocking the builder. Every follower must expect to be
cut adrift from his past, to "let the dead bury the dead";
he must be eager to put the call of his Master ahead of

his personal affairs; he must shoulder his cross and carry it. "Lo, we have left everything and followed you," Peter reminded his Lord. Jesus knew that they had, indeed, "left houses and brothers and sisters and lands" for his sake and the gospel's. He acknowledged their sacrifice. He had demanded it.

This costly personal attachment must be exclusive. Are we sometimes tempted by its severity to go away? At such times Peter's answer to the same question becomes our conviction: "To whom shall we go? Thou hast the words of eternal life" (A.V.).

When Cortez disembarked his five hundred conquistadors upon the eastern coast of Mexico, he set fire to the ships. His warriors, watching their means of retreat burning in the harbor, knew that they were committed with their lives to the conquest of the new world for Spain. All doubt had been cauterized from their minds. Similarly, everyone who first sets foot on the shores of discipleship is called upon to burn his ships in the harbor. In the call of Jesus to us there is something not unlike the marriage vow. There is nothing provisional about it. No trial period is allowed; no reservations are written in. It is a lifelong union for all the serpentine turns of fortune, "for better or worse, for richer or poorer, in sickness and in health." And it is exclusive: "Forsaking all others, wilt thou keep thee only unto him, so long as ye both shall live?" Out of such single-minded devotion a marriage is made; with anything less there can be none. Discipleship calls for all that marriage requires and more.

If we are disciples of Christ we are personally and sacrificially attached to him and to him alone. This allegiance is the commanding loyalty of our lives.

If we are disciples of Christ, we are also *learners* under the instruction of Christ. Quite literally, a disciple is a pupil, scholar, student or learner. In the Oriental world a teacher with his band of disciples was to that culture what schools and universities are to our society. And even in highly institutionalized forms of education everything else—books, administration, school buildings—exist only to do one thing: to bring learners into contact with teachers. At its core, education is still a log with Mark Hopkins on one end and a pupil at the other end. To be a disciple of Jesus is to go to school to him.

How fortunate it is that Christians were called disciples, rather than wise men or sages! Jesus once spoke of a scribe who became a disciple and thereafter brought forth out of his treasure things old *and things new*. Before his transformation, the scribe could have had little use for anything new. He was not a learner; he was versed in ancient truth, rooted in the past, quoting a revelation given once and for all on Sinai. He was an authority with a closed mind. What an irony of fate it was that these

learned authorities spoke without authority. But, no
wonder. They had confused a just reverence for truth
with their feeble apprehension of it. Truth, with a capital
"T," is undeniably eternal and unchanging; but truth as
grasped by human minds is a distorted view through an
imperfect mirror. We know in part. The Saintly Samuel
Rutherford dipped his pen in the ink of discipleship when
he wrote in one of his letters from prison: "How little
of the sea can a child carry in his hand; so little do I take
of my great sea, my boundless and running over Christ
Jesus."

In much the same spirit, the lyrical Francis Thompson
advised his friends that when they came to Heaven looking for him they should not search among the wise and
bearded counselors of God, but that they should go to
the nursery of Heaven. That is the only proper place for
any Christian—in the nursery, going to school in the
elementary department.

Notice some of the implications in our status as Christian learners. We must be on guard against errors in our
knowledge and idealism. What we take to be the mind
of Christ may very well be something less, or even contrary. Jesus had to rebuke the Twelve more than once:
"Ye know not what you ask!" They misunderstood him
during his ministry. What a difficult time he had stretching their minds up to the bigness of his teaching. And

the spirit of Christ went on stretching the minds of these men after the earthly Teacher has closed his instruction. Before the vision at Joppa, Peter stood with other Jewish disciples, fortified by righteousness, *against* Gentiles. It took a teachable man to learn another lesson and to be able to say, "Truly I perceive that God shows no partiality, but in every nation any one who fears him and does what is right is acceptable to him."

"Help me to discern my errors" is a fitting prayer for every disciple who is conscious of his involvement in a culture which is only half Christian. How easily he identifies the Christian view of man with rugged individualism or the Christian community with collectivism or makes western Democracy and Christianity identical terms. How gullible he is in seeking Christian approval for what Charles G. Shaw has denominated our "seven deadly values"—communication, speed, entertainment, health, psychology, sex, and youth. This pilgrim's progress of the modern secular mind may very well be the Christian's regress from the mind of Christ, needing the rebuke of Paul, "You did not so learn Christ!"

There is another implication. We must be open to the leading of Christ's spirit. The early church was very much aware of this leading. Witness the arresting words of the Fourth Gospel: "I have yet many things to say to you, but you cannot bear them now. When the Spirit of truth comes, he will guide you into all the truth. . . ." "Truly, truly, I say to you, he who believes in me will also do the works that I do; and greater works than these will he do, because I go to the Father."

A singular instance of this openness to the spirit of Christ is found in pastor John Robinson's advice to the Pilgrims as they departed from Holland. One of the *Mayflower* company reported, "He charged us . . . to follow him no further than he followed Christ; and if God should reveal anything to us by any other instrument of his, to be as ready to receive it as ever we were to receive any truth by his ministry; for he was very confident the Lord had more truth and light yet to break forth out of his holy word."

Can we see any of the rays of this new light penetrating the darkness of our strife-riven world? Yes we can, and some of its revelations are these: We must begin to be brother to our fellow human beings in the backward countries. We must learn how to fashion a concert of nations that will forever put an end to war. We must create in our own minds a new image of human community, to fill the place now occupied by our provincial national images of community.

As we are ready to learn and to follow, the spirit continues and will continue to guide us into all the truth. For if we are disciples of Christ we are under his instruction all our lives.

It is time that we attach ourselves to our Master and that we set ourselves to the learning of his lessons. We have fastened ourselves to other leaders of late; we have taken other lessons, with dire results . . .

> All our knowledge brings us nearer to our ignorance,
> All our ignorance brings us nearer to death,
> But nearness to death no nearer to God.
> Where is the Life we have lost in living?
> Where is the Wisdom we have lost in knowledge?[1]

Yes, where are the Life and the Wisdom? The disciple of Christ has his answer ready. They are found in the living, leading spirit of Jesus of Nazareth, who is the Way, the Truth, and the Life. An unknown poet voices the challenge:

> I heard Him call,
> "Come follow," that was all.
> My gold grew dim,
> My soul went after Him.
> I rose and followed,
> That was all.
> Who would not follow
> If he heard Him call?

---

[1] T. S. Eliot, *The Rock*. Copyright, 1934, by Harcourt, Brace and Company, Inc., and used by permission of the publisher.

II ✖ Brothers

But concerning love of the brethren you have no need to have any one write to you, for you yourselves have been taught by God to love one another; and indeed you do love all the brethren throughout Macedonia. . . . I THESSALONIANS 4:9, 10

We know that we have passed out of death into life, because we love the brethren. He who does not love remains in death.
I JOHN 3:14

CHRISTIANS today do not often call one another *brothers* and *sisters*. The practice, once so widespread in Protestant circles throughout America, has passed over to secular organizations—the fraternal orders and college Greek-letter societies. For example we are more frequently called *brother* in various chapter houses of our college fraternity than we are in churches. Modern Christians are not much given to calling one another *brothers*. And even before the practice died out, it was gradually being restricted to the clergy; church members called their minister *Brother Blank*, but they more often referred to each other as *Mister* and *Missus*.

Once it was not so. In the earliest days of the primitive church Christians called one another *brethren,* and referred to the church in a locality or throughout a whole province as *the brethren.* The title was well established as much as ten years before the disciples were first called *Christians* at Antioch, and still more years before they began to call themselves *Christians. Brethren* occurs no less than forty-five times in the book of Acts alone, and is repeated in the rest of the New Testament about a hundred times. It was a favorite name with our spiritual forbears.

There is a rich implication in the term that we ought not to lose in more modern days, for *brothers* is a word that has meaning only within a family. If men are brothers it is because, having a common parentage, they are members of the same family. This is what Paul meant when he wrote to the Thessalonians, "But concerning love of the brethren you have no need to have any one write to you, for you yourselves have been taught by God to love one another. . . ." If we are Christians, we are brothers, and if we are brothers we are members of God's family. This is one way of saying what a Christian is: A Christian is a person who lives as if he were a member of God's family. Notice what this insight does to one's point of view:

It makes him aware of the primacy of persons, and it

causes him to value persons above all other riches. In a family, persons come first. Wherever a house has really become the home of a true family, nothing is allowed to come ahead of the human beings who compose it—not the house itself, not the furniture, not the family fortune, not the regular income by which the home is sustained.

Take the simple matter of the health of children. Parents will undergo almost any sacrifice or privation to safeguard it, or to restore it when it is lost. We have seen men mortgage their houses to the eaves and borrow on their life insurance to the limit in order to provide six or seven months of skilled nursing and hospitalization for a child of theirs who was mentally ill. All of us know parents who have done things like this, and there are probably few of us who would not unhesitatingly do as much for our own children. Let possessions go, if only these loved ones can be won back to health. And if the health of their bodies is so precious, of how much greater concern are their moral soundness, their maturity as selves, and their usefulness to society. These we value beyond price.

Those who live in homes know that personality is literally priceless. How many times have we heard young parents say fondly, "Our Billy is only a little shaver, but we wouldn't take a million dollars for him!" They meant it, literally. Not all the gold buried at Fort Knox could buy one human being out of a genuine family from any member of that family. The world itself does not hold a sum of things precious enough for such a transaction.

What is true in the natural sphere for a human family is true for the Christian in the spiritual realm for the whole family of God. Persons come first for him and they are of unlimited worth. About a year ago in a Kentucky village I saw a bill of sale for a human being. Dated in the year 1855, the fading handwriting on this yellowing piece of paper showed just how one man made another man his slave by paying to a third party the sum of $800. By strange coincidence, shortly after seeing this bill of sale, one evening I opened *The Lexington Leader* to learn that one of the horse farms near the city had paid the fabulous amount of $400,000 for a French stallion. Immediately my mind flew back to the slavery transaction. "Four hundred thousand dollars for a horse!" I inwardly exclaimed, "and only eight hundred dollars for a human being!" I could not get the two contrasting sales out of my mind. What an inhumane inversion of values! And then I checked myself. Suppose the record had been reversed—$400,000 for the man and $800 for the horse— would that have righted things? Far from it. It would be as wrong to buy a man for $400,000 as for $800 because a human being, in God's world, should never be placed on the auction block. He is beyond price. He is worth more than the whole world, for he is my brother and he is a member of my family.

This judgment applies to all my brethren, for in a true family every member is priceless. The members of large families are not less bereaved by the loss of one than small families are. Every member is loved for himself and none can take his place.

Look at any real home and you can see this fact demonstrated, but it is difficult to extend the vision to the whole family of God. There it is easy to think that some human beings are expendable and that some are important while others are inferior. This is the natural view, but it is unworthy of men who have been born into the spiritual family. In his *Christ of Every Road,* E. Stanley Jones tells of an artist who had come to India to paint. He stood one evening in a small mission station, enraptured by the riotous color of a sunset splashed upon a bank of monsoon clouds. Deeply stirred, he could not restrain some expression of what he felt. "What a wonderful sunset," he exclaimed, "especially for so small a place!" As if God's sunsets acknowledged one part of the earth to be more important or more obscure than others; as though God could play favorites when he painted the twilight sky. No, God has no little places. And he knows no little people. All places are his, and among the children of men, all persons are his. As such they are our brothers. All of them are brothers of ours; they come before all other values and they are priceless.

What a benevolent check this personalism is upon our contemporary paganism. At a time when life is becoming more and more coldly impersonal, when "things are in the saddle and ride men," the Christian insight that we are brothers brings us back again to the hearth fire of a personal world. For the Christian, nothing should be allowed to have priority over persons—not economic profits, not national power, not any system or institution, and not even our ideas about persons. Nothing in this world should be allowed to seem to us more valuable than the children of men. When Jesus said, "The Sabbath was made for man, not man for the Sabbath . . ." he had in mind something more than the observance of one sacred day; he was publishing the principle of the sacred worth of human personality. Just as easily he might have said, "Man was not made for the economic order, but the economic order was made for man."

If we are Christians, we are brothers; and if we are brothers we are members of a spiritual family in which persons have primacy. But there is a twin truth to be seen here:

In a family, not only are the persons individually of unlimited worth, but they are bound together into a social whole; they are a community of affection. Brothers live together in love.

This does not mean that we must all be alike, that no

differences are to be allowed. Every parent sometimes remarks, "How different my children are from one another!" But no parent loves any child the less because he is different. Natural differences enrich a family. Far from being grounds for discriminations and exclusions, they are the source of fuller satisfaction. The solidarity of a home is not a level uniformity of sameness; it is a living harmony of differences.

So it is meant to be in the spiritual family for which Christians live. Human differences there certainly are; they are real and sometimes they are deep. We speak different languages, belong to different nations and cultures, are different in color, in education, and in economic privileges. These differences create tensions which now and then break out into open strife. It will not do for us to turn our backs upon them in a sentimental attempt to pretend that they do not exist. Nor do we need to expect that all will be peace and amity at all times, even within the church. Even the best of families sometimes break out in conflict, but in their altercations they know themselves to be together and they stay together working their way back to agreement and harmony. For such times great things are demanded of love: patience, unfading faith in others, humility and a forgiving spirit. No one has the family idea simply because he wants to make a family; he has to go beyond this to learn how to keep remaking it, reweaving its broken strands into the fabric of communal wholeness.

The Christian church from the beginning had worked at this task of bringing human differences into harmony. The Roman world was divided into slaves and masters. Some wanted to create unity by making masters into slaves. Others wanted to make slaves into masters. Christianity came along with a third alternative. It tried neither to make masters of slaves nor slaves of masters; it took both of them and made them brothers. Through the New Testament writings we catch now and then an intimate glimpse of this powerful harmonizing force at work. Here, for example, is Paul writing out of prison to Philemon, a master, pleading on behalf of Onesimus, Philemon's runaway slave. According to the code of the day, Philemon had the right to kill Onesimus as an example before other slaves, to keep them in their place. Nevertheless, Paul had the audacity to send Onesimus back to Philemon bearing a letter, and Onesimus had the courage to carry it by his own hand. "I appeal to you for my child, Onesimus, whose father I have become in my imprisonment," wrote Paul, as he went on to beg of the master that he receive Onesimus "no longer as a slave but more than a slave, as a beloved brother."

That same acid of brotherhood was eating away at other barriers of human discrimination and prejudice. It took the enmity between Jews and Gentiles and transmuted it into peace, not by turning Jews into Gentiles nor Gentiles into Jews, but by transforming both into Christians. It ate away at the wall of social station which separated the rights of men and women by inviting both to become full members of the human family. When citizens of differing nations abused one another by calling themselves "civilized" and labeling all other nationals as "barbarian," Christianity brought them together as citizens of the Kingdom of God.

No wonder the early Christians began to feel that they had been delivered from something deadly, and that in a day of dying culture they had begun really to live. "We know that we have passed out of death into life, because we love the brethren," said one of them. "He who does not love remains in death."

What the leaven of brotherliness began to do it has kept on doing, as it has honeycombed and toppled other dividing walls, and as it must in its nature keep on doing so long as humanity is divided against itself. Notice, for example, how this leaven has gradually abolished the distinction between the well bred and well born, on the one side, and the common people, on the other. Exploited and ground under by those who ruled by "divine right," the common people have been slowly rising in dignity for the past century and a half. It is not a very great exaggeration to call the twentieth century "the century of the common man," for nothing quite so exactly characterizes it as the rise of peoples all over the world to demand their elementary human rights. They rise as a mighty horde and they march as an irresistible multitude. They have found their voice, and they will be heard.

How foreign and remote to our present state of mind would an English parliamentary debate of 1807 sound in this present hour. It was in that year that a bill to provide elementary schools throughout England was defeated in the House of Lords. Both the Archbishop of Canterbury and the President of the Royal Society for the Advancement of Science voted against it. Upon what grounds? Because "it would teach them to despise their lot in life, instead of making them good servants in agriculture and other laborious employments to which their rank in society has destined them . . . it would render them insolent to their superiors. . . ." The strong wall which then separated the "superiors" from those whose lot in life destined them to be servants has been eaten into rubble by the acids of Christian humanitarianism.

Out of this growing insight there is emerging an increasing sense of responsibility. Men who are brothers feel responsible for one another. They begin to develop a social conscience. Albert Einstein gave voice to such a conscience when, during a stopover in China on a world tour, he refused to ride in a rickshaw because it was pulled by a human being. "I will not be a part of making any man a draft animal," he explained. Backward peoples in undeveloped areas who have been serving as the draft animals of white, Western civilization are now beginning to accuse the conscience of the world through the United Nations Trusteeship Council and other channels.

Sometimes we hear complaints against the work of relief and rehabilitation which the United States has been carrying on since the war: "We impoverish ourselves! We are ruining the country and wrecking our economic system to help other people. We'll soon be in the same boat with them, and then where will they look for help?" A touch of sober fact would soon silence such complaining. Glance at a few comparisons of the United States with twenty-eight undeveloped countries as they stood in 1949, according to the National Study Conference on the Church and Economic Life: In the United States the average man had at his command 37.6 horsepower; in the twenty-eight undeveloped countries the average horsepower per capita was 1.2. While Americans consumed 3,000 calories of food a day, these underprivileged natives eked out an existence on 1,800 calories. The average American income—counting women and children—that year ran to $1,300, while in these twenty-eight countries it amounted to only $100. When we realize that these cold statistics are pointer readings upon a boiling thermometer of human agony and injustice, we begin to feel ashamed of our complaining. As for the Christian, he will easily remember that somewhere it is written, "To whom much is given, of him will much be required."

Christians see themselves as brothers bound into a bundle of life with all other members of the family of God.

The Christian, living in an increasingly impersonal world, is committed to see things personally. He cannot see the earth as a world of things where men are competitors; he sees it as a community of persons, where men are brothers. Cain, who thought of himself as his brother's competitor, carried his false ideal to its logical outcome when he rose up one day and slew Abel. Then, through the torture of guilt and self-accusation, the voice of God spoke to him, but his spiritual ear was dull and he thought God was telling him that he was his brother's keeper. God was saying nothing of the kind. He did not want Cain to live as his brother's keeper. He wants no man to become a keeper for any other man. Such paternalism is short of true fraternity. Needy men who are dependent upon it are rightly resentful, like the Negro who flared up, "I don't want to be done good to!" No, what God was trying to say to Cain was simply this, "You are your brother's brother!" The Christian accepts this fact as life's true relationship.

Historians tell us that every Roman boy was taught by his pedagogue to say with the poet, "Remember, O Roman, thou art born to rule the world." The Christian has gone to another school, for down the Christian centuries Christ the master teacher has been saying to his disciples, "Remember, O Christian, thou art *born again* to be brother to every child of God."

III ✳ Believers

Now many signs and wonders were done among the people by the hands of the apostles. . . . And more than ever believers were added to the Lord, multitudes both of men and women. . . .

ACTS 5:12, 14

Now the company of those who believed were of one heart and soul. . . . ACTS 4:32

YOU have heard it said that people do not believe much of anything anymore. This may have been true for a short space following World War I, but it did not long remain so. Human minds find it difficult to sustain a spiritual vacuum. Men who have turned from the high challenge of cosmic religion have sought secular substitutes. Cleaving no longer to the Christian temple, they have built themselves synagogues of Satan. Harold Bosley put his finger on our malady when he said, "Unbelieving eras are cradles of new superstitions." Our modern mind is in no way unbelieving. It is a believing mind. It believes prodigiously. It believes in desperation. It believes uncritically. It believes in gods that are no gods. Because it has refused to become the captive of Christ, it is in the grip of monstrous new superstitions.

Striding through a Western city in the twentieth century, Paul would have cause no less than in first-century Athens to say, "I perceive that in every way you are very religious." The difference between Paul and his auditors, then and now, is not in religiousness, but in the object of worship. Belief in itself has no virtue; it is a human necessity.

There are beliefs that can make us children of hell. Jesus warned of this in so many words when he upbraided the Pharisees for their missionary zeal: ". . . you traverse sea and land to make a single proselyte, and when he become a proselyte, you make him twice as much a child of hell as yourselves." Some beliefs condemn us.

But there are also beliefs that can save us. Said Paul to his Philippian jailer, "Believe in the Lord Jesus, and you will be saved. . . ." The early Christians, who often called themselves believers, hazarded all on this faith.

Let us look at some of the beliefs that condemn us before we pass on to consider the faith that can save us.

There is the blighting faith in the sovereign state. That was a wise Christian statesman a number of years ago who called nationalism "Man's Other Religion"; and his observation is more nearly true today than when he made it.

We in our times have witnessed the emergence of the totalitarian state. The political arm of society has become the master of the whole social body, and even gives orders to the head and the heart. National prestige drowns out the call of humanity. Politics displaces morality. Force usurps the throne of truth. Back in the days of Fascist Rome, the ancient imperial city was plastered with posters bearing Il Duce's motto: "Believe. Obey. Fight." Believe in whom? In Il Duce! Obey whom? Il Duce! Fight for what reason? Because Il Duce commands it! We used to laugh in ridicule at the strutting figure of Mussolini. "Sawdust Caesar!" we jeered. Perhaps all Caesars are sawdust. That does not make them any less dangerous; in fact, that is their danger. They look for a time like leaders worthy of trust, but they are inwardly lifeless. It was just such a sawdust Caesar who taught his ruthlessness to Hitler and joined with him to lead a world to the slaughter pen.

This modern faith in the omnipotent state is a spreading contagion. In every country it takes upon itself as a disguise some costume native to that country and parades abroad as a saviour. Whatever its form, when the state becomes a mortal god without the chastening hand of the immortal God its power is a kingdom of hell.

One distinguished contemporary theologian, Emil

Brunner, has even gone so far as to say that the totalitarian state is *the* Satanic manifestation of our times.

Again, there is the disappointing faith in science as a messiah which has only so recently characterized Western society. There was a time, not long past, when it was almost universally believed that science would soon solve every riddle of existence and sit as king over every circumstance. There was some reason for such a belief. Power in ever-increasing magnitudes was being unlocked from the vaults of nature. Witness the mounting crescendo: water power, steam, electricity and atomic energy. Marvel at the near-conquest of disease, and the almost miraculous extension of the human life span. Only death and the weather seem reluctant to bow to the almighty sway of science, and even these have made concessions. "Rain-maker" is no longer a term equivalent to "witch-doctor"; it is a sober title for a man of science who has been able to demonstrate his powers, even by coloring the rain he makes.

All of this has given reason for believing in the power of science, but it has not given just cause for believing that science is all-powerful, nor that it could take over the whole province of human life, including that of religion and ethics. It is the essence of science that its knowledge is power, but science as such can give no judgment about the uses to which its power is put. Thus a scientist works with equal efficiency in producing radiant energy to treat blood cancer, or an atomic bomb to dissolve the blood of our national enemies. The latest triumph of science has revealed this ambivalent power, and its destructive possibilities have frightened scores of scientists back into a moral role. Twelve such men joined together in February of 1950 to issue a statement about the hydrogen bomb, reputedly a thousand times as destructive as the atomic bomb. These men had abdicated the role of scientists and were speaking as moralists when they said, "Its use would be a betrayal of all standards of morality and of Christian civilization itself." Speaking as "worried citizens," they continued, "We believe that no nation has the right to use such a bomb, no matter how righteous its cause. This bomb is no longer a weapon of war but a means of extermination of whole populations."

The greatest scientists have never made extravagant, all-encompassing claims for science. They have never said that it was a messiah. And now they are disabusing their mistaken worshipers who had imputed divinity to them. Clearly men arrayed with the power of gods and who are not controlled by the spirit of God are not something more than men, but something less. They are, as a contemporary religious journal has said, "devil-gods."

All that we have said about science applies to technology. It is a sobering realization to see that the Utopia of Francis Bacon in his *New Atlantis* was a society much like ours. In that island of the ideal, men would measure and predict the weather, control disease, travel under the sea and in the air. Presumably in that realm of applied science man would have arrived at the Good Society. So Francis Bacon supposed. But, now that Bacon's Utopia is no longer a dream but a concrete fact, we see that the Kingdom of God does not come by technology. We shall not be saved by the gasoline motor, nor by television. The good life is not an invention.

Another belief that may condemn us is the pathetic faith that a bullet can stop an idea. There are those who would meet a hostile faith with nothing but physical force. This is like fencing against weeds, or like discharging a rifle into a tornado.

Look more closely at this business of fencing against weeds. The only protection against the weeds of communism is the planting and cultivation of our own garden —the faith in and the practice of our Christian democracy. This does not mean that there will be no military fences. We will build fences against cows of imperialism, lest they come over and devour the garden. But we must not spend all our time building and guarding fences against the cows, else our garden will go to weeds through neglect, and there will be no continuing reason for the fence. It is the tragedy of our time that we have become a world of fence builders and that we are spending almost no time at all in the garden. Amid all this frenzy over military defenses, where is the passion for the faith and the practice of Christian democracy? Where is the concern for justice? What has happened to our compassion for the hungry and needy millions who compose two-thirds of humanity? Where are the gardeners?

Statism, scientism, technology-worship—these and other idolatrous beliefs would have attracted the eye of Paul walking through a modern city of our civilization. It doesn't require a very fertile imagination to hear him saying, "Men of America, I perceive that in every way you are very religious. For as I passed along, and observed the objects of your worship, I found also numerous altars . . . to an unknown God." What altars does he mean? What ones but our Christian churches? These are our tributes to a God we no longer know. We need someone to tell us, "What therefore you worship as unknown, this I proclaim to you."

"Believe in the Lord Jesus, and you will be saved. . . ." This was the saving faith of the first Christian *believers*. They could have said, "Our creed is Christ, and we have no creed but Christ." What did they mean?

Perhaps we can see their meaning against three possible views of faith. One view says that faith is a subjective mystical experience which I may have. It is my own, private. I cannot fully share it and I can never explain it. It is an ecstasy that only I may feel in just my way, an inner light that illumines only me. A second view says that faith is an authoritative statement of truth. Romanism took this view, finding the faith in official church pronouncements. Protestantism adopted it, defining faith as a set of orthodox opinions, supposedly derived from the Bible. Since the Bible supports no such view, the Bible alone was always regarded as too latitudinarian; therefore the faith of the Bible was defined and systematized in carefully worded Confessions of Faith and creedal statements. There is no real place in such a view for religious liberty. There is not even any real room in it for Christ, only for cold doctrines about him and hot strife to determine which set of doctrines shall prevail. Something must be wrong with such a view; as we watch biblical faith through the pages of the New Testament, we see it as faith that works in love, whereas creedal and dogmatic "faith" is something that more often festers in self-righteousness.

The faith of the early believers was neither of these. It had two foci, the person of Christ and the person of all who live as if Christ were Lord of their lives. A man might come to such a faith through intellectual assent, but the faith itself consisted in trusting oneself, mind and body and soul, to Christ. We may more easily understand what the first Christians were driving at if we exchange the words *belief* and *faith* for two other words, *loyalty* and *devotion*. For the Christian, faith is not something he can believe with his head and prove with his tongue. It will require all of him. When you came into church by answering *yes* to the question, "Do you believe that Jesus is the Christ?" what you should have meant was this: "I will live from now on with Christ in control of my life."

Of course such devotion rests back upon a conviction. This is the conviction that in Jesus of Nazareth we have a disclosure of cosmic power of basic reality. It is the assurance that in Jesus we have a demonstration of what is at once highest in spirit and deepest in nature.

There are tremendous implications in such faith. They call for great believing. They demand the risk and hazard of heroic hope. Look at only a few of these implications:

The highest ideals are the hardest realities. With Jesus the divine life stopped being a speculation and emerged on the plane of history as reality. Love burst upon the world both as tragedy and as the ultimate power. The historian Arnold Toynbee has said that the greatest new event of our time is still the Crucifixion, and the clergyman Ralph Sockman meant the same thing by other words, "The hinge of history is on the door of a Bethlehem stable."

With such a conviction rooted deep within their souls,

men are not easy victims of expediency or coercion. With such a universal absolute, they do not hear Truth speaking in national versions; for them it speaks a universal language. They are not quickly impressed by appearances nor easily cowed by the first easy victories of falsehood. They may have to pass through the valley of the shadow of death or mount the hill of tragedy, but they walk without faltering because they know whom they have believed and they are persuaded that this is a moral universe. They may not be able to *prove* this ethical insight as a logical proposition; but they have *seen* its moral power in Jesus and they will demonstrate it with their lives.

We are the children of God. Naturalism may speak of man on the spinning earth as "a sick fly on a giant flywheel," but the Christian faith knows that he is the child of God. "There is surely a piece of divinity in us," declared Sir Thomas Browne, "something that was before the elements and that owes no homage to the sun." This consciousness of standing before God gives the Christian the humility of human dependence and the dignity of divine descent. It shows him how to avoid self-idolatry and self-abasement, and it guards him from disillusionment.

History has a transcendental destiny. Much of this destiny is yet to be realized within history itself, but history cannot exhaust it; nor can history by its failures and frustrations invalidate the kingdom above history. It is time now that we return to belief in the immortality of the Christian soul implicit in the Resurrection of Christ. The Christian is one who firmly believes that the significance of life cannot be fully exhausted or completely exhibited in this world. This life in this world is tremendously significant, but The Life is immeasurably richer and larger. The Life fills this life, and overflows it, like the ocean filling a teacup dipped into its waves. Christians "have no continuing city" in the world; they are in it as "strangers and sojourners." Therefore they are able to pass through it without damaging entanglements, to face its defeats without despair, and go on hoping when others find nothing but grounds for despair.

The Christian walks under a divine word, like that delivered by Socrates to Glaucon at the end of Plato's *Republic*, "Wherefore my counsel is that we hold fast ever to the heavenly way and follow after justice and virtue always, considering that the soul is immortal and able to endure every sort of good and every sort of evil. . . . And it shall be well with us both in this life and in [the life to come]."

To be a Christian is to be a believer! Into a decaying Empire the early Christians hurled the creative deed of a daring faith. With bad news all around, they boldly believed in the good news which they read in Jesus. These "through faith conquered kingdoms, enforced justice, received promises, stopped the mouths of lions, quenched raging fire, escaped the edge of the sword, won strength out of weakness. . . ." What they did can happen again, if we only believe.

IV ⚹ Witnesses

But you shall receive power when the Holy Spirit has come upon you; and you shall be my witnesses in Jerusalem and in all Judea and Samaria and to the end of the earth. . . . ACTS 1:8

That which was from the beginning, which we have heard, which we have seen with our eyes, which we have looked upon and touched with our hands, concerning the word of life—the life was made manifest, and we saw it, and testify to it, and proclaim to you the eternal life which was with the Father and was made manifest to us—that which we have seen and heard we proclaim also to you, so that you may have fellowship with us; and our fellowship is with the Father and with his Son Jesus Christ. . . . I JOHN 1:1-3

IN THE twentieth century, *witness* is a word having a split personality. On the one hand it is a worldly habitué of the law courts, where witnesses give evidence during trials by judge or jury or affix their signatures to wills and affidavits. On the other hand, it is a pious, other-worldly creature giving intimate personal recitals of sin and grace in prayer meetings; or it is the zealot of a sect selling pamphlets about Armageddon on street corners or accosting strangers in sepulchral tones with the question, "Brother, are you saved?" These emotional colorations, secular or sanctimonious, insensibly mingle with the letters spelling out the word and make it distasteful to many, even in Christian circles. Some squirm in discomfort at the mention of it.

Nevertheless, witnessing, in the sense of testifying for a faith, is more vigorous than at any time in history, although we do not call it by that name. Today it is advertising, publicity, campaigning or propaganda. Whether it is the smooth voice of the radio announcer inviting us to "Smoke Smoothies," a giant picture of an automobile leaping out of the billboard, or "The Voice of America" beamed overseas, here we have the modern substance of the ancient term. This is witnessing—for profit, for defense, for rival faiths.

In this modern variety of testifying, of course, those who talk usually want something. So true has this become that we are developing some sales resistance and even some immunity to propaganda. An American tourist of Germany, for example, reported that as late as the summer of 1950 there were still some churches in the former Third Reich where congregations refused to listen to sermons; the spoken word, on the tongue of Hitler, had fallen so low that none could do it reverence.

All of this sort of reaction points up the imperative of

recovering witnessing in its original, Christian sense. In the beginning every Christian was a witness. By whatever name we choose to call it, witnessing is an activity integral to genuine Christianity. If we are Christians, we too have received the charge of our Lord: "You shall be my witnesses in Jerusalem and in all Judea and Samaria and to the end of the earth." What are Christian witnesses?

A witness, in the root meaning of the term, is a person who is present when something important happens. He is one who has personal knowledge of an event and who can talk of it out of his own firsthand experience. A Christian witness is, therefore, one who has personal knowledge of Christ. He is one who has seen and heard and touched the reality of the Christian faith, through a face-to-face encounter.

For an insight into such an encounter let us look outside of Christianity, at the recent conversion of the American journalist Vincent Sheean to whom we have already referred in our first chapter. In his visits with Gandhi, Sheean said, he had learned "that a man must at all times be ready to give his life for his truth. It involves a great decision, which, once made, can never be retracted." This personal insight grew directly out of what Gandhi had done in his own life, for "Gandhi had himself decided long ago and since then had never been afraid."

Then Sheean goes on to relate his personal reaction to

the shooting of Gandhi, which he saw with his own eyes. He says that he was in the grip of a deep emotion, deeper than any he had ever known. He can only describe it, he writes, as a storm in the head: "I felt the consciousness of the Mahatma leave me—I know no other way of expressing this: he left me." This internal sensation was accompanied by two physical ones: "Then I was aware of two things at once, a burning and stinging in the fingers of my right hand and a similar burning and stinging in my eyes. The tears, he says, were not ordinary; they were much more acid than usual. And the blister on his finger was large and painful for days.

In review, what do we see as the essential lines of this indubitably religious experience? A complete analysis would require a text in the psychology of religion and not a little reverence for mysteries too vast for human comprehension, but at least three things happened: (1) Sheean was present at an event in which he felt personally involved. He had identified himself with Gandhi to such a degree that he entered into his mind and spirit and into his sufferings. He was not only present at the martyrdom, he was in it, on the inside of the tragic deed, at one with the martyr. (2) Sheean saw that he had to make a decision which would involve a death to his old way of believing and a surrender to the faith which he had seen in his hero. He saw that "a man must at all times be ready to

give his life for his truth." Here was his great decision;
once he had made it he felt bound to it. (3) New insight
and assurance then began to flood his soul. He knew himself to be a different man, in a new relationship to the
world.

It must have been in much this same way that the early
Christians thought of themselves as witnesses of the Crucifixion and the Resurrection. They too were drawn by the
grace and truth which they saw in Jesus. They were present *in* the martyrdom; the sword reached into their very
souls. The Resurrection, likewise, was so internal to them
that it was difficult to tell just where feeling left off and
fact began. These were deep inner cataclysms in the souls
of men as well as in the sphere of outer events. The men
who experienced these things knew themselves to be in
the presence of demands; it became imperative that they
make decisions, whereupon they changed their minds
(repented), and died to their old lives in order to come
into their own resurrections (were baptized). Then came
the flooding reality of new insight and assurance. Never
had they experienced things as *real*. They felt themselves
to have seen deep into the heart of things. "We have
heard, we have seen [it] with our eyes; we have looked
upon it and touched it with our hands, and we have found
it to be the word of life!" they exulted.

Now, what about us? Can we too be witnesses of the

Resurrection? Someone will protest, "How can we? The event is over and done with. An impassable gulf of time denies us admission to it." Admittedly our experience of Christ cannot be as direct. It may also be less ecstatic, but we can have it through the mediation of Christian personality and history.

How are we drawn to him? Through Christian persons we have known who have taken on some of the qualities that the contemporaries of the disciples discerned in the Twelve. And we also "took knowledge of them, that they had been with Jesus." Undeniably this is the first and strongest force that draws us to Christ. We walk to our Lord over a bridge of human hearts spanning the centuries. But there is more. Christian history, through the New Testament, has given us the words and deeds of Jesus so that we can know what manner of man he was; it has also given us the epic story of the work of the risen Christ in his body, the church. Moreover, when we are discerning, we can detect the touch of Christ upon our civilization—in the emancipation of women, the enlightenment of universal education, the humanitarianism of medical science, the internationalism which calls to our warring world more and more insistently, and the Christian personalism which focuses the light of divine glory upon the faces of the common people. Humanitarianism, internationalism, enlightenment and personalism—these are the marks of our Lord branded into the body of our civilization. Thus he is lifted up, and so he draws us to him.

It is not enough to be drawn by such an attraction. A man must answer when he is called. Having seen in Jesus the truth, "a man must at all times be ready to give his life for his truth. It involves a great decision, which, once made, can never be retracted." Then he is ready to say, "I have heard, I have seen it with my own eyes, I have looked up at it and touched it with my hands and I have found it to be the word of life." He is an eyewitness of the truth.

A witness, in a secondary meaning of the term, is one who tells what he has seen. What his eye has taken in, his tongue then proclaims. Thus, a witness is not only one who sees an event, but he is one who testifies to it. A Christian witness is, therefore, one who communicates his personal faith to those who have not yet received it.

We return to the experience of Vincent Sheean. Once he was in possession of his new faith, having passed through the personal cataclysm which we have already described, he felt driven to tell somebody about it. Almost compulsively, therefore, he crossed the street in front of his New Delhi hotel and entered the nearest house, which happened to be that of an acquaintance, Jai Prokash, a leader of the Indian Socialist Party. "He was sitting on the floor by a long open glass door through which the sun, warm that day, was flooding in. I sat on the sill and talked to him.

"I have rejected historical materialism once and for all," I said, "I believe in God."

The early Christians felt the same compulsion. It was not that Christ had commanded them to tell others, nor that they felt constrained by the duty of evangelism; it was that they *had* to tell others. The news tumbled out of them in gladness. They could scarcely restrain it. One gets the impression from the book of Acts that there were no places and no times in which the early disciples did not engage in witnessing. In temple and at home they shared their story. They told it in synagogues and on journeys. Through sunlit days of popularity with the people, and equally under the cloud of persecution—in court and in prison—they continued to tell it. They told it when they were together in close-knit companies, and when they were scattered as lone individuals and as tiny bands of refugees. Lone evangelists taught lone individuals, as Philip instructed the Ethiopian eunuch. Apostles, two by two, stood in assemblies and taught crowds, as Peter and John continued to do through many days in the temple. These same apostles met with households.

Such unrelenting proclamation bears results. The people were convinced by it, so that thousands believed and were baptized. Even those who did not believe were fascinated. There was such evident personal earnestness here, such clear sincerity, such an impression of reality. Officialdom, in its own way, was just as deeply moved. It was moved with apprehension over the damage that these followers of the executed Nazarene would do. It was appalled by the number of people who were being swept into the heresy; and it gave grudging testimony to the power of the disciples' proclamation: "You have filled Jerusalem with your teaching," its spokesmen said.

When Saul of Tarsus fell upon the Jerusalem church with his fiery inquisition, the ensuing explosion of persecution spewed disciples out of Jerusalem in all directions. No doubt many of them returned to their former homes, in Galilee, Damascus, Cyprus, Phoenicia, Rome, Alexandria, and in the nearer towns of Judea and Samaria. We shall never know the extent of this early dispersion, since Acts is not a comprehensive history, but we do know that the disciples were scattered "as far as Phoenicia and Cyprus and Antioch" and "throughout the region of Judea and Samaria." Many who returned to their homes must have taken believing citizens of Jerusalem with them as traveling companions and houseguests.

"Now those who were scattered went about preaching

the word." Persecution had not shaken the faith of the saints. They were as determined and loyal as they had been in Jerusalem. In fact, the dispersion offered them a new and fruitful field for evangelism. Here were their old Jewish friends and neighbors who had not yet heard the Galilean story; here were new acquaintances with eager ears. Thus it came about that most of the disciples did more than remain loyal to their new faith; they won converts and allies to it in new places, and the movement took root almost simultaneously in towns and cities far removed from one another.

Such is our heritage and example of witnessing. It was done fervently and continuously, but it was also done through natural channels. Friend talked with friend, kinsman with kinsman, neighbor with neighbor. Meetings already assembled for religious purposes, and having provision for laymen to speak, gave other opportunities. Witnessing was done normally and naturally.

Unnatural, highly sentimentalized and sanctimonious ways of telling the story usually repulse more people than they convince. For example, a friend of mine tells of being a passenger in an airplane bound from the United States to Puerto Rico. Early in the flight a black-garbed woman in her middle years walked to the front of the plane and began to speak. She explained that she was answering a private call of God to go to Puerto Rico as a lone, independent missionary and while on her way she did not want to lose an opportunity to testify for her Lord. She then displayed a little black book. "See," she said. "This book is bound in black. That is the sinful condition in which many of you live." Then she opened the book to some pages of red paper. "This," she said, "is the blood of Christ which takes away our sin." Then, turning to white pages, she said, "And here we are, when we have been washed in the blood of the Lamb." All on board the plane were embarrassed and alienated by the performance; none was converted, or even attracted. What was wrong? Among the several unnatural elements we single out these: The self-appointed missionary had taken unfair advantage of her hearers; if any person representing another faith or a commercial product had done the same, she herself would have been offended. She had spoken to a group of strangers about whom she knew nothing and without having taken the pains to discover anything; she did not know them as persons and she was not interested in them as persons. Her message was not geared to or stated in terms of the experiences of her hearers.

Though we are constrained to be witnesses for Christ, we are not required to shed our common sense nor to immerse ourselves in sentimentality. We cannot, in all reverence, burst into the citadel of a human soul before we have been invited in off the doorstep.

But within the normal relationships, among those we

know and who like and trust us, we have an inexhaustible opportunity to testify on behalf of our faith.

Moreover, the impulse to share must surely drive us to extend this influence to the ends of the earth. Missionaries and missionary societies and literature are the long arm of our personal influence, borne by our dollars, if not by our own words. Armed with science and skill, these missionaries have learned how to find and to use the natural channels for the communication of their precious truth. Now that the secular religion of communism has also become so fervently evangelical, our world is at stake. Upon the vitality, the constancy and the outreach of our Christian witness there depends nothing less than the destiny of Christian civilization. If the "Old, Old Story" is not to fade out of the world's life, we must tell it. And we must tell it where men are, wherever they are.

A Christian is a man whose tongue is aflame because his eyes are alight with the truth which he has seen. ". . . the life was made manifest, and we saw it, and testify to it, and proclaim to you the eternal life which was with the Father and was made manifest to us—that which we have seen and heard we proclaim also to you, so that you may have fellowship with us; and our fellowship is with the Father and with his Son Jesus Christ."

V ✳ Saints

Here is a call for the endurance of the saints, those who keep the commandments of God and the faith of Jesus. . . .

REVELATION 14:12

So then you are no longer strangers and sojourners, but you are fellow citizens with the saints and members of the household of God. . . . EPHESIANS 2:19

YOU are a Christian, aren't you?"

"Yes. At least, I try to be."

"Then you are a saint."

"What?"

"I said, you're a saint. To be a Christian means to be a saint."

"Who, me? Goodness knows, I never claimed to be a saint. I hope I'm a Christian, as far as that goes, but I don't expect I'll ever make enough headway at it to be enrolled with the saints."

A fragment of conversation like this comes out of a culture infused with the medieval view which divides

Christians into "seculars" and "the religious" and which reserves the title of "saint" for a select few, like St. Francis Assisi, from the whole body of Christians, whose self-denial and spirituality are far above us. From among the millions of Christians, according to this view, only a handful are elevated to sainthood.

This is not the biblical view. Paul called all Christians *saints*. It was his favorite name for them, in fact. He applied it to the whole church without distinction. He did not withhold the title even from the members of that quarreling, disorderly, problem-infested church at Corinth. Before launching into a disciplinary letter in which he upbraided them for sexual sin, for drunkenness, and for factionalism he addressed them in this way: ". . . to those sanctified in Christ Jesus, called to be saints together with all those who in every place call on the name of our Lord Jesus Christ, both their Lord and ours." If a man is a Christian, according to Paul, he is a saint.

The English term is a translation of three biblical words, two of them Hebrew and one Greek. The Hebrew *hasidh* means "one who is filled with love and loyalty to God"; *qadhash* means "the loyal ones." The Greek *hoi hagioi* may be translated "those who belong exclusively to God." It follows, then, that a Christian, being a saint, is to be counted among the loyal ones, who love God, and who belong exclusively to him. And this is the serious intention, not of a few rare souls, but of all Christians!

More specifically, what does it mean to be counted among the loyal ones who love God and who belong exclusively to him? Our answer follows some lines suggested by Douglas V. Steere in his book *Beginning from Within*.

In his demand for a better world, the saint begins with himself. This is a reversal of the usual way of going about social reform. "Why don't *they* stop all this injustice?" we generally ask, meaning by *they* the captains of industry, or the President and Congress, or someone else sufficiently remote from us and our position to give us a feeling of self-righteous irresponsibility. If, as may happen, we do occasionally perceive that we ourselves are involved in the network of injustice as pensioners of an evil system—like distillery workers or repairmen of gambling devices—we still try to put the task of building a better society on the shoulders of others. We excuse ourselves. We say, "If I don't do this, somebody else will! So even if I gave up my income from an industry of which I do not approve, I would not even make a dent in the system!" Whichever road I take, whether that of self-righteousness or that of expediency, I end up at the same place: "Why don't *they* do something about it?" I do not see that a better world begins with me.

But that is precisely what the saint does see. His prayer

is, "O God, create a new world, beginning with me!" He is willing to start alone and to take the risk of his venture. He knows that there will be no increase of justice unless someone somewhere takes it upon himself to make a modest beginning at the task, and he is able to see no reason for excusing himself from this responsibility. It is not his to argue that he is only a drop in a bucket; it is his to inquire what is right. It is not his to calculate consequences; it is his to do his duty and to leave the outcome with God. The Quaker Joseph Hoag was addressing a London audience in 1812, pressing home his urgent claim for converts, when a man from the audience cried out, "Well, stranger, if all the world were of your mind, I would turn and follow after!"

To this Hoag quickly rejoined, "So thou hast a mind to be the last man in the world to be good. I have a mind to be first." A saint has a mind to be first.

A saint is a person who has learned something about the power of one life. In a world worshiping hundreds of horsepower, he is a stranger and sojourner who has respect for one manpower. He looks at history and he sees tall men standing astride the crossroads of destiny. Plato and Columbus and Bacon and Ford and Einstein—and Hitler and Stalin—were all men like ourselves, with like passions and capacities, living in the same world with the same twenty-four hours to each day. The only difference is that each of them became the conscript of a dream and gave himself without reservation to a mission which claimed him absolutely. The destiny of the world, for good or ill, is enfolded in the lives of persons. There is no searching of the deep powers hidden away there and no measuring of such energy once it is released upon the world.

When, in 1945, the President of the United States made a radio broadcast reporting the use of the atomic bomb at Hiroshima, he said of this new weapon that it had released "the basic power of the universe." To this observation the poet Hermann Hagedorn wrote a telling rebuttal in the form of a prophetic poem, "The Bomb That Fell on America." Here he said that the atom was the greatest power in the universe, save one, "That one is the human soul." The poet went on to observe that this magic power of giants could be managed only by a people morally mature and that the urgent times demand that we shall grow up overnight. But where is this growing up to begin?

The Lord, he looked at me and His eyes pierced like hot wires. "Perhaps," He said, "there's something in you and numerous others that will have to be cracked open, if a hundred and thirty-five million people are going to grow up overnight. "Something in you," said the Lord, "something, perhaps in *you*." That *was* a joke, and I laughed. But the Lord wasn't laughing. I hastened to reassure Him. "There's nothing the matter with *me*.

It's the other fellow that's the trouble, a hundred and thirty-five million of him."

"I know all about the hundred and thirty-five million," said the Lord, and I thought He looked a little tired as He said it, "but I don't at the moment seem able to see anyone but you."

. . . .

"If I could get by your ego and somehow crack open your nucleus —Something might happen . . . And there is a world at stake."

. . . .

"Give me your life and I will make it a spade to dig the foundations of a new world, a crowbar to pry loose the rocks, a hoe to mix sand and cement, a trowel to bind stone and stone and make them a wall.

Man without God is a bubble in the sea, a single grain of sand on an infinite beach.

God without man is a mind without tongue or ears or eyes or fingers or feet.

God and man together, we are such power as not all the atoms in all Creation can match!"

The poet's answer to this godly challenge was a saintly response, for it was a simple surrender of one soul:

I laid my hand there in the hand of God[1]

The saint is, moreover, conscious of himself as a member of a minority. He associates with others who have surrendered to God's will. Nowhere in his letters does Paul speak of an isolated, individual saint. He always assumes that they are grouped in churches. This "fellowship of the concerned," as one contemporary has called

[1] Hermann Hagedorn, *The Bomb That Fell on America*. Copyright, 1946, by Hermann Hagedorn, and used by permission.

it, is a minority in any community; but standing over against man's majorities, it is God's minority.

History moves forward in the wake of spearheading minorities. The Christian movement itself began with one man, Jesus of Nazareth, who gathered twelve men about him and left at his death "a multitude"—notice the absurdity of the word—"a multitude of about one hundred and twenty persons" who, according to Acts tarried in Jerusalem. It was not long until the one hundred and twenty were five thousand, but the five thousand were still a minority measured against fifty million inhabitants of the Roman Empire. But that minority captured that Empire.

What is more, the redemption of a decaying order can never be the work of a majority. Majorities can muster political power, financial power, or even the power of armies, and these powers can multiply and extend the existing order; but they cannot redeem that way of life. What is wanting for that task is moral power, and this is to be found internally in the few who value the call of God above every other vocation.

Was this what Jesus had in mind when he called his disciples "the salt of the earth"? Salt seasons and savors, but only a little of it is required; a pinch of salt will season a whole kettle of food. Another of Jesus' favorite metaphors means much the same thing: Disciples as "the light of the world" do not have to be numerous in order to pierce the darkness; they only need to be aflame with God. In the recent war the blackout taught us the carrying power of the thinnest sliver of light. Even the tiniest beam can become a direction finder in the trackless night. It can show the way, though it be little.

The eye of faith, peering into our decaying civilization, will see something not disclosed to carnal eyes. It will see the saving power of a consecrated minority. It will see our proud civilization as a modern Gomorrah, needing only ten righteous men to stay the rain of fire.

Social conservation may rest in the hands of the majority, but social creation and redemption are left for other hands. These godlike labors can be achieved only by God's minority.

The saint has learned this; what is more, he has acted upon his conviction.

Not only does the saint begin with himself and associate himself with others willing to make such a beginning, but he has staying power. He has a kind of "holy stubbornness."

For one thing, he is not swept off his feet by opposition. He finds himself under divine constraint to belong in the succession of an embattled Peter and John standing before the tribunals of state, resisting threats, enduring the lash, and suffering prison without yielding ground. "We must obey God rather than men" is the only answer they can return to the demand for a lesser obedience. A Hitler, styling himself *The Leader*, confronts a Martin Niemoeller with his human sovereignty, but Niemoeller demurs, "God is my Leader!"

The apostles expected such endurance of their converts. "Stand therefore," Paul exhorted the Asian Christians. "Stand therefore, having girded your loins with truth, and having put on the breastplate of righteousness. . . ." It was important to him that they should be "able to withstand in the evil day, and having done all, to stand."

Engraved on front of the imposing memorial building housing the log cabin in which Abraham Lincoln was born near Hodgenville, Kentucky, are these extracts from his political speeches: "Let us have faith that right makes might, and in that faith let us to the end dare to do our duty as we understand it." So he had spoken at the Cooper Institute in New York, February 27, 1860. And at Peoria, Illinois, on October 16, 1854, his high integrity had found expression in a like statement, also engraved on this memorial to his birthplace: "Stand with anybody that stands right. Stand with him while he is right, and part with him when he goes wrong." Looking at the lowly log dwelling within that stately monument, the modern spectator may wonder what spark of divinity ever prompted a frontier lad to such a noble faith and enabled him to remain true to it. He had firmness in the right as God gave him to see the right.

There is, however, an even more difficult manifestation of staying power. This is patience for the long pull, where there is no opposition. It is unheroic faithfulness, "living to God in small things," which makes up the fabric of the daily Christian lives of most of us. Human beings have a remarkable capacity for rising to a crisis. Unsuspected heroism lies within the most prosaic of breasts to be drawn out by massive danger. There is scarcely a village anywhere in the world that did not watch some easygoing, soft-spoken youth depart from the comforts of home to do amazing deeds of valor in the recent war. "Who would have guessed that Johnny possessed such courage and self-forgetfulness?" No one has guessed, least of all Johnny. But the uncommon challenges of the battle line had drawn them out of him. But, whereas Johnny rose to these heights in one brief campaign, he returns home to live through the months and years an unchallenging life of nagging selfishness and petty irritation! Where is his courage for the commonplace?

Courage for the commonplace does not rise from the dimensions of an outward crisis; it is inwardly generated by a vital faith. Having its source in the perennial spring of a believing heart, it remains faithful through every circumstance. In seasons of adversity and of public favor, through hours of ecstatic vision and months of dull and burdensome duty, through praise and blame, and through indifference the saint stands by his faith. As Paul adjures Timothy: "I charge you in the presence of God and of Christ Jesus who is to judge the living and the dead, and by his appearing and his kingdom: preach the word, be urgent in season and out of season . . . be unfailing in patience. . . ." It is because he is aware of standing in the presence of Christ, because he measures all things by Christ and his kingdom, that he has developed the capacity to endure.

It is precisely because the saint, having ears, does hear the whisper of God, and having eyes, does see the handwriting of God, that he is able to withstand the common allurements of pagan conformity. Men pipe to him, but he does not dance; they wail, but he does not mourn. He is listening to another monitor. "If men do not keep step with their age," said Thoreau, "perhaps it is because they hear a distant drummer." The staying power of the Christian saint, carrying him through opposition and through the unheroic commonplace, is his response to the drumbeat of eternity.

More than eighteen hundred years ago the Seer of Patmos issued the summons, "Here is a call for the endurance of the saints, those who keep the commandments of God and the faith of Jesus." Millions have answered that call and left us their heritage—a Christian civilization. And now we are passing through a world revolution, testing whether that civilization, or any civilization with the Christian faith, shall endure. A chapter is closed. The earlier Christianization of a pagan world has turned, in our time, into the paganization of the Christian world. There is nothing to reverse the tide but a resurgence of spiritual energy. There must be some courageous souls who will make a beginning at the only place where they can be sure of controlling something in this world of demonic forces—with themselves. We must have souls who will not be ashamed to stand in the right with a few, and who will have the holy stubbornness to remain faithful unto death. "Here is a call for the endurance of the saints—those who keep the commandments of God and the faith of Jesus."

VI ⚹ Children of God

Beloved, we are God's children now; it does not yet appear
what we shall be, but we know that when he appears we shall
be like him, for we shall see him as he is. . . . I JOHN 3:2

For all who are led by the Spirit of God are sons of God . . .
it is the Spirit himself bearing witness with our spirit that we
are children of God, and if children, then heirs, heirs of God
and fellow heirs with Christ, provided we suffer with him in
order that we may also be glorified with him. . . .

ROMANS 8:14, 16, 17

ONE of the most poignant scenes in all literature is
that incident at the end of Plato's dialogue the *Phaedo*,
where the friends of Socrates are gathered around him in
prison while the fatal hemlock is dragging him down
into the clutches of death. A member of the group regis-
tered the enormity of their sorrow in these words: ". . . he
was like a father of whom we were being bereaved, and
we were about to pass the rest of our lives as orphans." In
the twentieth century many have suffered an even blacker
bereavement; they live in the world bereft of a heavenly

Father, and they pass their lives as the orphans of the universe.

For Christians this is not so. Born of the spirit as well as of the flesh, they "have received the spirit of sonship." They do not cry out into the stars, "O thou cold and limitless space!" or "O thou blind force!" but they do cry, "Abba! Father!" For us Christians, "it is the Spirit himself bearing witness with our spirit that we are children of God." There is assurance and warmth in the affirmation, "Beloved, we are God's children now; it does not yet appear what we shall be, but we know that when he appears we shall be like him. . . ." Hidden deep within this consciousness of divine sonship, there are three gems of insight.

The first of the insights reveals our human dignity. If we are the children of God, we are his offspring and we are in some degree like him.

We might suppose that man would have greater dignity without God. Humanism has tried that. It has celebrated man's power to make himself, to advance his society through reason, and to conquer nature by science. Auguste Comte, the French sociologist, even carried this praise of man to the extreme of worship. He founded the Religion of Humanity, prepared a calendar of sacred days and a canon of humanistic saints, formed a cultus and organized a church, confident that this new faith in the self-sufficiency of man would soon sweep the earth. It did nothing of the kind; instead, it flourished as a nine-day wonder and then as quickly subsided into impotence and oblivion.

Humanism may *begin* as a modern Hamlet celebrating human nobility: "What a piece of work is a man! How noble in reason! how infinite in faculty! in form, in moving, how express and admirable! in action how like an angel! in apprehension how like a god! the beauty of the world! the paragon of animals!" But it is a curious paradox that this same modern Hamlet soon finds himself overpowered by disillusionment and futility: and he, like his original, *ends* his song of praise in a whimper: ". . . and yet, to me what is this quintessence of dust? man delights not me; no, nor woman neither, . . ."

The whimper of Hamlet is echoed everywhere that the cult of Humanity has said its ritual: Will Durant says, "God, who once was the consolation of our brief life, and our refuge in bereavement and suffering, has apparently vanished from the scene. . . . Life has become a fitful pullulation of human insects on the earth, a planetary eczema that may soon be cured; nothing is certain in it except defeat and death—a sleep from which, it seems, there is no awakening."

Robert Louis Stevenson in *Pluvis et Umbra* reports another echo: "What a monstrous spectre is this man, the disease of the agglutinated dust, lifting alternate feet or lying drugged with slumber; killing, feeding, growing, bringing forth small copies of himself; grown upon with hair like grass, fitted with eyes that move and glitter in his face; a thing to set children screaming. . . ."

The quest for human dignity without God ends in a parching desert of disillusionment. Humanism breaks itself against the solid reality of the universe. Man is not God; he is the child of God. If he tries to become a god he will degrade himself into a demon. Such is the paradoxical truth: ". . . for every one who exalts himself will be humbled."

In his novel *The Vintage* Anthony West draws a picture of hell as a fair country and of Satan as an urbane and sophisticated gentleman by the name of Ransome. One morning Ransome and the principal character of the story, Wallis, are sitting on an outside balcony overlooking the country. Ransome sits with his back to the rail, but Wallis faces out, searching the horizon for a second glimpse of the hazy mountains that he had seen at dawn the day before just for an instant. He had come to suspect the truth that early in the dawn of the first days in that deceptive country men see hazy mountains on the horizon and then lose sight of them. There is hope for men, as long as they can see these mountains, and they can make their escape. But later when they have stayed too long, they cannot see the mountains at all, and they are trapped forever. As they sit on the balcony Ransome chides Wallis for searching the horizon for the mountains; he assures him that there are no mountains. "Man is nothing but the sum of his thoughts and actions," he says. "What you have here [in this country] is man in his own image, there's nothing else." But Wallis resists such reasoning; after all, he *had* glimpsed the hazy mountains. He knows that they did exist. He cannot wholly desert the conviction that man is in the image of God; suddenly he remembers the lines of the poet Dante: ". . . deny not, to this so-brief vigil of your senses that remains, experience of the world without man that lies behind the sun. Consider your nature, you were not made to live like beasts, but to pursue virtue and knowledge."

Man is not merely man; he is the child of God. There is something more than his own image of himself to steer by. If he will accept his true status as a child, he is elevated to godlike dignity. "He who humbles himself will be exalted."

"What are we?" asks Thomas Wolfe in one of his poems. Throughout the verses he keeps fumbling for an answer which he reaches in these closing lines:

> We are the sons of our father,
> And we shall follow the print of his foot forever.[1]

---

[1] "What Are We?" from *A Stone, A Leaf, A Door*, selected by John S. Barnes (Scribner's). Copyright, 1945, by Maxwell E. Perkins and used by permission of the publisher.

The second insight reveals our human dependence. If we are the children of God, we need him as an infant needs its parents.

This dependence of man upon God is not inconsistent with human dignity. It is, in fact, the root and source of that dignity. Human dignity without human dependence is a futile tower of Babel erected out of pride and pretension. It aims at setting man upon a throne in heaven; it ends by hurtling him into earthly confusion and slavery. It is not dignity as a god that man should seek; that is impossible to him. It is dignity as a man; and that he may have if we will admit his dependence as a child of God.

President John Mackay of Princeton Theological Seminary recently located the difficulty, "Made in God's image and God-likeness being his true nature, man has sought to become like his Maker, not, however, as his Maker's creature and child, but as his rival. He has wanted to be 'like God' by becoming self-sufficient and independent of God. . . . In order to carry out his own will, he has wanted to be a god." Dr. Mackay has translated the Tower of Babel into modern language.

As God's offspring, man is like, but he is still a child, a creature and not the Creator. Instead of seeking to be like God in power so he can do his own human will, he must seek to do God's will, so he can be like God in spirit.

Once a man has accepted his dependence upon God as

a fact, he begins to discover unimagined sources of enjoyment and of energy. He is suddenly like a swimmer who stops struggling against the lake and lets the water buoy him up naturally. He is like a plant that spreads its leaves to the warmth of the life-giving sun and sinks its roots into the soil of the nourishing earth.

He sees the world differently. Every earthly thing takes on a heavenly radiance. Every human thing has a divine significance. The world is no flat, two-dimensional tableland; it is a three-dimensional sphere; to every human measurement God is added. We do not see a universe of black and white and intermediate gray; when we look with eyes of the children of God we see a universe in technicolor!

> Not where the wheeling system darkens,
> And our benumbed conceiving soars!—
> The drift of pinions, would we hearken,
> Beats at our own clay-shuttered doors.
>
> The angels keep their ancient places;—
> Turn but a stone and start a wing!
> 'Tis ye, 'tis your estrangèd faces,
> That miss the many-splendoured thing.[2]

He walks among men with a different kind of confidence. He gains the power of independent judgment, and

[2] Francis Thompson, "In No Strange Land." (Published posthumously.) Used by permission of Burns, Oates & Washbourne, Ltd.

if he must stand out against a human majority for a conviction, he can do it because as one who stands alone with God he becomes a spiritual majority in his own right.

No longer conforming to the expectations of men, he is no longer frightened into polite conventionality and useless mediocrity. Instead, the work of transforming his mind into the mind of Christ and human society into the Kingdom of God elevates him into a spiritual aristocracy.

He undertakes tasks too ambitious for the children of men. He cannot see the distant scene of moral duty; nevertheless, he sets out for it by taking the next step in the duty that lies nearest him, trusting to the kindly light to reveal the next step, and the next, and to lead him to the true city of the Good. He is surrounded and even almost overwhelmed by the Kingdoms of this World, but he continues to dream about and to labor for the Kingdom of God. And he dares to do this because he trusts his Father. "The way of man is not in himself, that it is not in man who walks to direct his steps." "Commit thy way unto the Lord; trust also in him, and he shall bring it to pass" (A. V.).

The third insight reveals the path and the goal of our destiny. "Beloved, we are God's children now; it does not yet appear what we shall be, but we know that when he appears we shall be like him. . . ." If we are the children of God, we must grow toward godlikeness.

We human beings are like children living in an adult world. The doorknobs are just beyond our reach, the table is so high that we cannot see what is on it, the chair so heavy that we cannot lift it. A child must feel very much as the true scholar feels in a public library; here are thousands or even millions of books of which he can read only a few hundred in a lifetime; he clutches at the whole domain of learning with infant hands which can hold so little. Or here is a scientist who can make only a little inroad of light into a whole continent of human ignorance. His steps of knowledge are toddling and uncertain baby steps.

Paul Elmer More, the classical scholar, took note of this uncertainty: "We are intellectually incompetent and morally responsible. . . . We are born knowing nothing and with much striving we learn but a little; yet all the while we are bound by laws that hearken to no plea of ignorance. . . ."[3] "Such knowledge is too wonderful for me; it is high, I cannot attain unto it." Much more simply Paul says the same things for all of us in other words, "I can will what is right, but I cannot do it." By this he does not mean that we can do nothing right, but that we

[3] Paul Elmer More, *Pages from an Oxford Diary* (Princeton University Press, 1937).

cannot do all the right. In the realm of morals we are children.

Under such circumstances the only realistic virtue is humility—the humility of the child who asks his father to lift him into the high chair or to answer a question that he cannot solve alone; the humility of the scholar who acknowledges his debt to thinkers before him and leaves his unfinished task to thinkers who shall follow him; the humility of the scientist who seasons all his affirmations with questions and resists dogmatism with an open mind. Pride might be a fitting virtue for a race of supermen; but in men who are children it is a vice. "In such a state humility is the virtue of men," continues Dr. More, "and their only defence: to walk humbly with God, never doubting, whatever befall, that His will is good, that His law is right."

And the only proper outcome is growth. If we are children, then our most serious business is that of growing up. Do you ever wonder why living in an adult world does not completely discourage children? You might think that forever reaching for doorknobs that they cannot grasp, tiptoeing at tables too tall for them and tugging at objects too heavy for them would frustrate them entirely; but it does exactly the opposite. It fills them with a passion to grow up. In the moral universe something very like that ought to happen to every child of God.

As a growing person, the Christian faces a future containing a more mature self and a nobler humanity. This faith in the possibility of growth into an unlimited future even crosses the frontier of death.

Such a faith is wholly other from the dusty doubt that corrodes the pagan mind. An English churchman recently observed that "Christianity was born into a world that was haunted by the conviction that man was about played out." More than a few traces of this haunting conviction are to be found in Jewish literature. Take, for example, this quotation from the Second Book of Baruch:

> . . . the youth of the world is past
> And the strength of creation already exhausted
> And the advent of the times is very short,
> Yea, they have passed by;
> And the pitcher is near to the cistern
> And the ship to the port
> And the course of the journey to the city
> And life to its consummation.

To this senile humanity, death is the crowning indignity, a final and irrevocable defeat. "Brief and powerless is Man's life; on him and all his race the slow, sure doom falls pitiless and dark. Blind to good and evil, reckless of destruction, omnipotent matter rolls on its relentless way. . . ." is the dirge of Bertrand Russell, a modern. A Jewish sage, Jeshua, son of Sirach, dolefully said something very like it two thousand years ago:

> . . . the breath in our nostrils is smoke,
> And the reason is a spark in the beating of our hearts;
> When it is quenched, the body will turn to ashes,
> And the spirit will dissolve like empty air. . . .
> And our life will pass away like the traces of a cloud,
> And be scattered like mist
> Pursued by the sun's rays. . . .[4]

For the Christian, the child of God, this is an absurdity. He is not senile, even at the end of his earthly life; neither does he believe that humanity is about played out. The world to him is not an old folks' home adjacent to a graveyard; it is the Nursery of the Universe. "Beloved, we are God's children now; it does not yet appear what we shall be, but we know that when he appears we shall be like him. . . ."

Over against the people who pass their lives as orphans of the universe, the Christian is a person who is conscious of living as a child of God. He has the dignity of divine descent, the humility of human dependence, and he strives in hope toward a godlike destiny.

[4] The Wisdom of Solomon 2:2-4. *The Apocrypha, An American Translation,* by Edgar J. Goodspeed. Copyright, 1939, by the University of Chicago Press.

VII ✻ Stewards

As each has received a gift, employ it for another, as good stewards of God's varied grace: whoever speaks, as one who utters oracles of God; whoever renders service, as one who renders it by the strength which God supplies; in order that in everything God may be glorified through Jesus Christ. . . .   I PETER 4:10, 11

This is how one should regard us, as servants of Christ and stewards of the mysteries of God. Moreover, it is required of stewards that they be found trustworthy. . . . I CORINTHIANS 4:1, 2

And the Lord said, "Who then is the faithful and wise steward, whom his master will set over his household, to give them their portion of food at the proper time? Blessed is that servant whom his master when he comes will find so doing." . . .

LUKE 12:42, 43

IN THE middle of the twentieth century a Christian has to make his way against two false views of money and things. First there is the secular fallacy, implicit in much advertising, that a man's life does consist in the abundance of the things he possesses. Would he have a full life? Then let him acquire automobiles, TV sets and electric shavers. Having acquired them, let him keep replacing them with later, improved models. If the good life never quite seems to materialize and if happiness evades his grasp with serpentine elusiveness, it is always possible to assume that he does not yet own enough things or that he has failed to acquire the right things. Then there is the religious fallacy, implicit in much so-called "steward-ship," to the effect that a Christian has done all that God requires of him when he has given away a portion of his income to the church and to charity. This portion can be any reasonable amount, but at its upper limits it should never be more than a tenth. This tenth, moreover, will be given only by those ambitious to attain superior righteousness!

These two fallacies support each other: A Christian, justifying his conduct by them, can be pagan in the acquisition, ownership and use of his money so long as he gives a small percentage of it "to God." Thus it is not necessary to renounce mammon in order to worship God. Rather, the world can be neatly divided between the two deities—10 per cent God, 90 per cent mammon.

How shall the Christian resist the almost overpowering tug of these fallacies? He can do it only by broadening his conception of stewardship. *Steward,* an Anglo-Saxon word, is a compound of *stig*—meaning *house* or *hall*—and *weard* —*warden* or *manager.* Thus a steward was an employee who served as the manager of a wealthy man's house or estate. He did not own the estate, but he controlled it as a trust to be discharged in the interest of the owner. A Christian steward therefore regards the physical world as God's estate which he manages in trust according to the will of God.

If a person is a Christian he is Christ's steward. This means that he conducts all his material affairs for the glory of God through the service of mankind. Not alone his giving, but also his acquisition, ownership and use of money and things will be offered as spiritual service. Not a dollar of his nor a thing he owns will be withheld, and no department of his material affairs will be immune to the scrutiny of Christian conscience. All his material affairs will be conducted for the glory of God through the service of mankind.

What is the role of a Christian steward in the acquisition of money and things? John Wesley once preached a now-famous sermon on "The Use of Money" which he based on Luke 16:9: "And I say unto you, Make to yourselves friends of the mammon of unrighteousness; that, when ye fail, they may receive you into everlasting habitations" (A.V.). Wesley reduced his instruction on this text to three plain rules: "Gain all you can, Save all you can, Give all you can." His first rule did not mean, however, that a Christian should gain all he can by whatever method; rather "we ought to gain all we can gain, without buying gold too dear. . . ." When is the price of money too high? When it hurts one's own Christian conscience and harms his neighbor. In its lefthanded way it says that to a Christian some things are more precious than money—his own physical and mental health, his integrity and the welfare of his neighbor. If he has to sacrifice any of these for material gain, he is "buying gold too dear."

This leads us inevitably to a consideration of vocation, for it is through their callings that most men acquire money. A vocation must be considered positively. It is not enough to view it negatively, as Wesley did, saying that all gain is legitimate which does *not* hurt the conscience or harm one's neighbor. What positive requirements must it fulfill? Service. Creativity. Harmony with the will of God.

Service to our fellow men comes first because money is a social symbol—a recognition of an exchange of goods for services rendered. But even here the Christian will approach service somewhat differently from the non-Christian. He will see that it is possible to serve the *wants* of men while rendering a disservice to the men themselves, as in narcotics traffic or commercialized gambling. He will aim, therefore, to serve genuine needs in such a way as to contribute toward the full realization of selfhood for everyone whom his occupation touches.

Creativity follows close upon the heels of service, because a man ought to serve through that occupation which gives the widest scope to his own unique talents. A man ought to experience achievement in his work, to be fulfilled by doing it, to grow as a person because of it. We should ruin no skillful carpenters to make inept schoolteachers. No natural-born lawyers should have to drudge through an unpleasant existence as bankers.

Both service and creativity should be in harmony with the will of God, and that will can be known through the revelation of the Christian gospel. In fact, it is the Christian faith itself that often sets the task through which service is rendered and on which creativity is expressed. Teachers, nurses, librarians and missionaries all serve in occupations which would not have existed or would have been obscure and marginal except for the concerns generated by religious faith.

It all comes to this: A person's occupation should be chosen and filled as a part of his Christian stewardship. He should acquire money in ways that are incidental to the service of mankind, and to his realization of complete selfhood, in ways that are consistent with his Christian understanding of himself and of his neighbor.

All of this stands in black-and-white opposition to the pagan acquisition of money for its own sake or for the sake of what it can buy. Such acquisitiveness is seen by

the Christian through the eyes of *Koheleth*: "He that
loveth silver shall not be satisfied with silver; nor he
that loveth abundance, with increase; this also is vanity.
When goods increase, they are increased that eat them;
and what advantage is there to the owner thereof, save the
beholding of them with his eyes?"

The Christian also finds himself deeply in sympathy
with a brief recital of manual trades by Jeshua, son of
Sirach, in his apocryphal book *Ecclesiasticus*. After de-
scribing the work of the plowman, the carpenter, the
smith and the potter, he goes on to pay them this tribute:

> All these rely on their hands;
> And each one is skillful in his own work;
> Without them, no city can be inhabited,
> And men will not live in one or go about in it.
> . . . .
> They do not sit on the judge's seat,
> . . . .
> Yet they support the fabric of the world,
> And their prayer is in the practice of their trade.[1]

Here are the three qualifications of the Christian steward working at his vocation: he is skillful at his own work;
he helps to support the fabric of the world, and his work
is a prayer lifted to the throne of God.

What is the role of the Christian steward in the ownership of property?

___

[1] Goodspeed, *op. cit.*

The original draft of the preamble to the Declaration of Independence is said to have read that "men are created free and equal and endowed by their Creator with certain unalienable Rights, among which are Life, Liberty and *Property*. . . ." The Christian will recognize this legal right to human ownership, but he will never regard it as absolute. He believes instead with the Psalmist that

> The earth is the Lord's, and the fulness thereof;
> The world, and they that dwell therein.
> For he hath founded it upon the seas,
> And established it upon the floods.

Starting from acknowledged ownership of God over the whole physical universe including his money, his property and his own body, the Christian goes on to remark that the attempt to usurp God's title and establish undisputed human ownership over anything is disastrous to men. Without God, men do not possess their possessions; they are possessed by their possessions. "There is a grievous evil which I have seen under the sun," observed the disillusioned Old Testament sage, "namely, riches kept by the owner thereof to his hurt. . . ." Apparently our age is not the first time in history that "things are in the saddle and ride men."

The French philosopher Rousseau, in fact, saw private property as the serpent in the Garden of Eden. In his *Discourse on the Origin of Inequality* he wrote:

The first man who, having enclosed a piece of ground, be-thought himself of saying *This is mine,* and found people simple enough to believe him, was the real founder of evil society. From how many crimes, wars, and murders, from how many horrors and misfortunes might not anyone have saved mankind, by pulling up the stakes, or filling up the ditch, and crying to his fellows, "Beware of listening to this imposter; you are undone if you once forget that the fruits of the earth belong to us all, and the earth itself to nobody."

While we feel no attraction to Rousseau's splendid savage living in a primitive, communal society, we should like to agree with him that the secular belief in *private property* does lie at the base of endless crimes, wars and murders, horrors and misfortunes. Human ownership of property, unmodified by the sovereign ownership of God, is not a safe idea to release among men.

The Christian steward is cautious, therefore, in using the word *mine*. He does not try to drive permanent stakes to enclose as his a piece of land which was there before there was ever a human habitant and which his last descendant must leave behind when he goes to his long home. He will think of his legal property as a trust and of himself as God's trustee; this inward image of himself will affect everything that he does about the material universe, beginning with that part of it nearest to him—his own body, which he will now see not as his to abuse at will, but as the temple of God's spirit. As for his property he will think less of that than of his manner of using it in the service of man for the glory of God, knowing "as he came forth of his mother's womb, naked shall he return to go as he came, and shall take nothing of his labour, which he may carry away in his hand" (A.V.). What then can he take? Nothing but the mantle of his stewardship!

A Christian steward must have a care about the spending of his money. This includes the spending of all his money, even that for groceries and clothing. He knows that he can serve God not only by the way in which he acquires it and holds it but also by the manner in which he lets it go.

Some usage of money is waste. "Do not throw the precious talent into the sea; leave that folly to heathen philosophers," Wesley advised in the sermon on "The Use of Money." "Do not throw it away in idle expenses, which is just the same as throwing it into the sea." Wesley went on to counsel a little more austerity than any of us would like to practice:

Expend no part of it merely to gratify the desire of the flesh, the desire of the eye, or the pride of life. . . . I do not mean, avoid gluttony and drunkenness only: an honest heathen would condemn these. But there is a regular, reputable kind of sensuality, an elegant epicureanism, which does not immediately disorder the stomach, nor impair . . . the understanding; and yet . . . it cannot be maintained without considerable expense. . . . Waste no part of it in curiously adorning your houses; in superfluous or expensive furniture; in costly pictures, painting, gilding, books; in elegant rather than useful gardens. . . . Lay out nothing to gratify the pride of life, to gain the admiration or praise of men.

While most of us feel Beauty is one of the daughters of God along with Goodness and Truth, we cannot gainsay Wesley when he insists that luxury can be quickly and easily overdone. The Christian steward will know how to scale down his private wants. He will not squander his income on himself. He will live with a greater degree of simplicity and austerity than his pagan neighbors.

Those who attended Yale Divinity School in the 1930's will remember the strong influence exerted over them by a professor who lived by such a rule of austerity. He rented a house in a section of town where the rents were lower; he drove nothing but a secondhand car for which he refused to pay more than $150. He wore $4 shoes and a $25 suit. With these economies he was able to live on $2400 a year and to give the remainder of his $5,000 salary to charity. He did all of this because of a very sensitive social conscience. Luxury, he felt, was theft of bread from the mouths of the hungry. Who can say that he is not upheld by the conscience of Christ? Showy houses, ornate houses and expensive clothing do not seem consistent with the service of the lowly Carpenter of Galilee who lived so compassionately in the midst of needy, suffering humanity.

The Christian steward will also be on guard against supporting antisocial forces through his spending. Let him look out upon the predatory influences in his society: yellow journals, gambling, prostitution, alcoholism, racial discrimination. Then let him ask himself, "From how many of these evil forces have I withheld the support of my own spending?" Some indulgences, taken on an individual scale, seem harmless enough, but when magnified to social proportions through the like indulgence of millions they become monstrous. How many damaging influences are there in our world which would wither if they depended on your support? This is one test of your Christian stewardship.

"Who then is the faithful and wise steward, whom his master will set over his household, to give them their portion of food at the proper time? Blessed is that servant whom his master when he comes will find so doing . . ."

As John Wesley admonished, the Christian steward will give all he can. Giving will not be the whole of this stewardship, as some have mistakenly supposed. Some have seemed to think that giving is always meritorious, no matter how the money was acquired. So it is—but how much good does it accomplish, erasing as it does a part of the wrong that was created by unchristian methods of acquiring it? The Christian will take care to see that all parts of this Christian stewardship pull together. His acquisitions of money will not work against his charity; nor will his possession and spending of money belie his giving. Giving is not the whole of his stewardship, but it is an important part of it. Therefore he will give.

He will give from motives of humanitarian concern. "But if any one has the world's good and sees his brother in need, yet closes his heart against him, how does God's love abide in him? Little children, let us not love in word or speech but in deed and in truth."

He will give as he is able—having, in fact, made himself able through careful spending. The advice of Paul to the Galatians will find lodgment with him, "So then, as we have opportunity, let us do good to all men, and especially to those who are of the household of faith." Whether his opportunity is to give much or little will not primarily concern him, for he will know that God sets requirement only in terms of abilities.

A current report from the Twentieth Century Fund does not show us living up to these opportunities in terms of our abilities: "Organized religion and private social welfare represent a relatively small and apparently declining share of our economic life. It appears that consumers have devoted to the support of the church and welfare institutions little more than $1.50 out of every $100.00 of their expenditures in recent years. This is considerably less than we spend for either tobacco or alcoholic beverages." This is a dismal regression from the Old Testament religion that spoke of "tithes *and* offerings"; such giving represents neither tithes nor offerings; it is only a collection.

Giving has little to do with amount but a great deal to do with spirit and sacrifice. The most touching story on the subject in the New Testament is that of the widow's mite. Similar incidents have inspired thousands and brought millions of dollars into the treasury of the Lord. There was, for example, that time in 1880 when the Disciples of Christ were lingering overlong on the threshold of a genuine foreign missionary program, although their Foreign Christian Missionary Society had been in existence since 1875. J. H. Garrison, one of the two leading journalists of the brotherhood at that time, was preparing to depart for the 1880 national convention in Louisville, Kentucky, when two of his small sons[2] and a girl cousin brought him the contents of their savings banks and said, "We want this to go to send the gospel to children who have never heard of Jesus." The amount of their contribution was exactly $1.13, but it was the beginning of Children's Day among the Disciples, which has financed scores of missionaries in ten foreign fields over a period of more than sixty years. Here is the miracle

[2] One of the sons was W. E. Garrison, present literary editor of *The Christian Century*.

of the loaves and fishes translated into currency. God is always performing this miracle for those who have the widow's consecration or the Garrison boys' complete and believing unselfishness.

The Christian steward will give. He will give sacrificially, proportionately, regularly and cheerfully. He will give as a natural outgrowth of his Christian faith and for the purpose of a larger domain in this world for the Kingdom of God.

To be a Christian a person must work out a Christ-centered solution of the problem of things. He must acquire, possess and use them as a part of his Christian vocation; and he must share them in Christian giving. To rise to such a height, as Martin Luther said, "every man needs two conversions: the first of heart and the second of his pocketbook."

VIII ✳ God's Elect

43619

Ye have not chosen me, but I have chosen you, and ordained you, that ye should go and bring forth fruit, and that your fruit should remain. . . .   JOHN 15:16 (A. V.)

Put on therefore, as God's elect, holy and beloved, a heart of compassion, kindness, lowliness, meekness, longsuffering. . . .
COLOSSIANS 3:12

But ye are an elect race. . . .   I PETER 2:9

I N THE New Testament, Christians are often called "God's elect" or some like title to indicate that they are *a chosen people*. Many of us, reared in a non-Calvinist tradition, have been embarrassed by these passages. To be quite frank, we may have wished that they were not in the Bible. Such emotionalized thinking springs, of course, from the identification of *election* with certain popular, other-worldly notions of *predestination* and *fore-ordination* having to do exclusively with heaven and hell. These notions find expression in many old creeds, like that of one local church on the Western Reserve in 1825, which read, in part:

"We believe that before the world began, God did

elect a certain number of men unto Everlasting Salvation, whom he did Predestinate to the Adoption of Children by Jesus Christ."

From such a dogma it follows that God also foreordained a certain number of men from the foundation of the world—even before they were born—to eternal damnation. We are further instructed by some of these old creeds and confessions of faith to believe that the number of the elect and of the damned could not be altered by so much as one human being.

"If this is the doctrine of election," we have said, with no little moral indignation, "we unconditionally reject it!" It seems hideous to us, for it makes God cold and despotic; it denies human freedom, and turns all man's religious strivings into an empty formality.

Nevertheless, after the emotional storm has cleared, it still remains true that the New Testament speaks of Christians as "God's elect." We have no choice but to accept the title and to look more closely into its original meaning.

The New Testament usage rests upon the Old Testament doctrine of the chosen people. Prophetic teachers from the eighth century onward learned to make a distinction between Israel after-the-flesh and the True Israel of the faithful. The earliest Christians, falling right into this way of thinking, identified their movement with the doctrine of the remnant, the True Israel about whom the prophets had spoken. There was at the beginning no notion on the part of any of the apostles that the new movement was anything separate from Judaism. It was a national call to repentance, an enrollment of flesh-and-blood Israelites among morally obedient Israelites-indeed, who were simply asked to accept Jesus of Nazareth as the complete fulfillment of their agelong Messianic hopes.

But two things happened to alter their original view. First, the Jews did not respond as the apostles had expected. Second, non-Jews, who were not originally in the plan at all, began to respond; and they responded in such numbers that the followers of Jesus had no choice but to think of themselves as a new people. In time, distinguishing themselves from both Jews and Gentiles, they began to label themselves the Third Race. Before this development took place, however, an intermediate one intervened. The Christians began to think of their movement as the New Israel, successor to the Israel of Canaan.

In no place is this view of the New Israel more clearly set forth than in Paul's figure of the wild olive branch which was grafted into the domestic olive tree—the wild branch representing Gentile Christians. "But if some of the branches were broken off, and you, a wild olive shoot, were grafted in their place to share the richness of the olive tree, do not boast over the branches. If you do boast, remember that it is not you that supports the root, but the root that supports you." When, at a later date, the writer of the First Letter of Peter addresses the Church as "a chosen race," although he is speaking to an audience which is predominantly non-Jewish, he is thinking in Jewish terms, of a New Israel.

It follows, therefore, that a sound doctrine of the chosen people for the Old Testament will throw light on the New Testament doctrine. The Israelites themselves were tempted to distort their election into a demand for divine favoritism. They expected moral immunities. They anticipated political advantages. They awaited a golden age based on plunder and privilege.

The prophets were quick to denounce such mistaken dreams. "Woe unto you that desire the day of the Lord!" Amos thundered. "Wherefore would ye have the day of the Lord? It is darkness, and not light." Election interpreted as special privilege could lead only to disaster. Carl Sandburg was writing in the best tradition of the prophets, as a kind of twentieth-century Amos, when he penned his "Four Preludes on Playthings of the Wind" in which he said essentially the same thing:

It has happened before.
Strong men put up a city and got
   a nation together.

And paid singers to sing and women to warble: We are the
    greatest city.
  the greatest nation,
  nothing like us ever was.

And while the singers sang
and the strong men listened
and paid the singers well,
there were rats and lizards who listened
. . . and the only listeners left now
. . . are . . . the rats . . . and the lizards.[1]

It was in this spirit that Jeremiah in the seventh century B.C. prophesied doom against the Temple. "Judgment begins at the house of God." The election of the
Jewish people meant not extraordinary privileges *but*
extra demands of moral uprightness.

However, if Israel had been elected to nothing more
than moral righteousness, she could have become a nation of self-righteous Pharisees, glorying in moral superiority to the rest of mankind. Election, therefore,
meant something more than a call to righteousness; it
also involved a summons to service. Centuries were required to refine this idea in the fires of national hardship
through which the Jews passed, and even after the idea
emerged it seems to have remained the conviction of a
minority. Nevertheless, it is now quite generally con-

[1] From *Smoke and Steel*. Copyright, 1920, by Harcourt, Brace and Company,
Inc. and used by permission of the publisher.

ceded that the loftiest conception of a nation to be found in the Old Testament is that of Israel as the suffering servant. It was in the fifth century B.C. that the peerless unknown prophet of Babylon lifted his song of service, whose undying melody haunts us still: "Thou art my servant; Israel, in whom I will be glorified. . . . I will . . . give thee for a light to the Gentiles, that thou mayest be my salvation unto the end of the earth."

When the prophet penned these words his people were in exile, their backs bowed under the service of triumphant Babylon. Rising above resentment and homesickness, the unnamed seer had the grace to see that God had meant Israel to be the servant of the nations and that this enforced servitude was a divine reminder in-the-midst-of-judgment of what he had called his people to do freely out of their own hearts. This was the first glimmering vision of the truth that "he who is greatest among you shall be your servant; whoever exalts himself will be humbled, and whoever humbles himself will be exalted."

The Second Isaiah combined historical realism with spiritual insight when he saw that Israel's moral service to the rest of mankind involved a complete repudiation of the normal patterns of imperialism and power: "Behold, my servant, whom I uphold; my chosen, in whom my soul delighteth: I have put my Spirit upon him; he

will bring forth justice to the Gentiles." But not by vio-
lent means! Not through political sway! "He will not cry,
nor lift up his voice, nor cause it to be heard in the street.
A bruised reed will he not break, and a dimly burning
wick will he not quench: he will bring forth justice in
truth. He will not fail nor be discouraged, till he have
set justice in the earth; and the isles shall wait for his
law."

The normal patterns of imperial power were repudiated for the elect nation by Second Isaiah. But that was
not all. He went further, the whole length to the insight
that a way of humble service had involved and would
continue to involve suffering, which suffering was a redemptive ministry to the world: "Surely he [the suffering
servant, Israel] hath borne our griefs, and carried our
sorrows; yet we did esteem him stricken, smitten of God,
and afflicted. But he was wounded for our transgressions,
he was bruised for our iniquities; the chastisement of our
peace was upon him; and with his stripes we are healed."

We now have the full picture of Israel's election from
among the nations. It was an election to a high moral
integrity (sealed in a covenant), to the role of patient
advocate of justice among the nations, and of vicarious,
suffering service on their behalf. The chosen people were
chosen to live God's righteousness, to spread his justice,
meantime bearing within themselves the pains of such

a mission to an ungrateful and misunderstanding world.

One more element is needed to complete the Old Testament picture. Within the chosen nation individuals were often elected to special tasks. Moses and the prophets were *called,* or elected. To what were they eleced? Not to a privileged position; not to power. Rather, they were elected to duties and services which were at first repugnant to them and which most of them tried to escape. They were elected to deliver unpopular messages, to suffer social ostracism—in short, to serve God at staggering personal cost. And most of them who were called had the intuition that the cause which they served was, for their day at least, foredoomed to be a lost cause. A study of the calls of the prophets is exceedingly rewarding. They remind one of Abraham Lincoln's joking comparison of his galling public office with the tarred and feathered victim of a mob who was being ridden out of town on a rail and who was saying, "If it weren't for the honor, I'd rather walk." There was little honor but much hardship in the life of those persons whom God elected to special services. They were not elected to office; they were elected to a task.

"If God's choices of men recorded in the Old Testament, by which the Christian doctrine of Election was suggested, are examined, they prove to have been choices of men to his service; selections of persons to do certain works for him and accomplish certain purposes; elections of men not so much for their own benefit as in order that through them certain ends of God might be wrought out." This is theologian William Newton Clarke speaking in his book, *An Outline of Christian Theology*. He continues, to amplify his definition by illustrating it: "Thus Abraham . . . was chosen and called out for the sake of the world and the future; Jacob was chosen that through him the line of blessing might proceed; Joseph, that the way of his family in Egypt might be prepared; Moses, that Israel might be brought out of Egypt. . . . Israel itself as a people, that the nations might have a witness of the living God among them." Then Dr. Clarke makes this clarifying generalization: "According to the teaching that runs through the Bible, no one was chosen primarily for his own sake or advantage, but all were chosen for service."

We ought to say, of course, that the service to which the Christian is called is not charity in its modern sense. There is no condescension in the service of Christ, no handing down of gratuities. Rather, the spirit of Christlike service is seen in the kneeling Master, washing his disciples' feet. From such a position he can look up into their faces.

We now have before us the full doctrine of election. If Christians are a chosen race, God's elect, they are called

out of the world. The Greek word for *Church* says this
literally; they are called away from secular moral standards to God's measures of right. They are called, not to
privilege, but to humble service of humanity. And the
constant reminder of this call is found in their Lord, who
"came not to be served but to serve, and to give his life as
a ransom for many."

With a twinkle in her eye and a playfully superior air,
a church woman recently said, "Isn't it nice that we are
among God's elect!" She was being facetious, but if she
had been serious, the answer would have been, "No, it
is not nice to be among God's elect. It is frightening; it
is awe-inspiring. It may even be glorious. But it is not
nice." There is something in all of us which resists such a
call. We may want to be called out of the world to a
moral island far removed from the world's corruption or
into a tiny community of privilege, but we mightily resist being called back into the world as its servants. Excuses leap to our lips, excuses which echo the reluctance
of other chosen ones in the long ago: "Who am I that I
should go. . . ?" We protest that we are without elo-
quence, nobodies having scant influence, just as Moses pro-
tested. "I am a man of unclean lips. . . ." With Isaiah, we
argue that we are not good enough for a duty so lofty.
"Ah, Lord Jehovah! behold, I know not how to speak;
for I am a child." So now we enter Jeremiah's objection:

we are not wise enough for so urgent and demanding a
time! But God thinks as little of our arguments as he did
when they were on the lips of Moses and Isaiah and Jeremiah. "Say not, I am a child"; he replies to our excuses,
"for to whomsoever I shall send thee thou shalt go, and
whatsoever I shall command thee thou shalt speak."

To be called out into superior light is to be called back
into augmented responsibilities. A saving withdrawal
from society is for the purpose of a redemptive return
into the thick of it. Plato saw this in the fifth century B.C.
He set it forth largely in terms of *wisdom* in his celebrated myth of the cave in the seventh book of the *Republic*. Picturing ordinary men as prisoners chained in
a cave with their backs toward the light and their faces
toward the wall, whereon they see nothing but shadows
which they mistake for realities, Plato then releases one of
these benighted souls into the outer sunlight. At first
he is blinded by the sun and bewildered by real things,
having been accustomed for so long to the dark and to
his familiar world of shadows. Then, after a time, he
gets adjusted and begins to revel in his freedom and
knowledge. The last thing he wants is to be sent back into
the cave. He himself will not like the darkness now after
the light nor enjoy the shadows after experiencing
realities, nor the chains after the freedom. Moreover, his
former fellow prisoners will not welcome him gladly

when he tells them that theirs is a world of shadows, for they ignorantly suppose it to be real; they may even hate him and kill him for his pains. Nevertheless, Plato insists, the wisest and best men of the state "must continue to ascend until they arrive at the good; but when they have ascended and seen enough we must not allow them to do as they do now."

"What do you mean?"

"I mean that they remain in the upper world: but this must not be allowed; they must be made to descend again among the prisoners in the den, and partake of their labours and honours, whether they are worth having or not." For, said the wise Greek, philosophers were created not to please themselves but to be God's instruments in the state, binding it into a harmonious whole.

A clergyman who recently took the lead in cleaning organized crime out of a city in western Kentucky and who endured anonymous threats upon his life, was asked how he had got into the crusade. "I got tired hearing myself talk and decided to see whether I meant what I was saying," was his reply. He had crossed over from his moral island to the mainland into the thick of dangerous service, having resisted the challenge until his self-respect could stand it no longer without loss. This is the universal experience of all who are truly called of God—reluctance, even resistance, giving place to yielding in the face of

God's mandate. Jeremiah's bit of autobiography is as typical as any other: "O Lord, thou hast persuaded me, and I was persuaded; thou art stronger than I, and hast prevailed. . . . And if I say, I will not make mention of him, nor speak any more in his name, then there is in my heart as it were a burning fire shut up in my bones, and I am weary with forbearing, and I cannot contain."

Turn now to another implication of our call. *We are also called to salvation, but our salvation is to be found in our service.* Put it another way: We are saved by faith, but faith is a commitment that has no substance apart from works. If salvation is not to be an otherworldly affair, a bookkeeping transaction in heaven having to do only with the residential address of souls after death, it must rise above the legalism and magic of fiat into the dynamic reality of a process. Such a view discards the doctrine of an arbitrary election to salvation and damnation. Rather, it finds salvation through service. God calls men to serve, and as they serve they are saved—paradoxically, without intending to save themselves at all. "For whoever would save his life will lose it, and whoever loses his life for my sake will find it."

We are dealing here with a spiritual principle which seems also to be mirrored in natural law. Blessings when received but not worked for can spell death. Recently in the vicinity of St. Augustine, Florida, great flocks of sea gulls were reported to be starving in the midst of plenty. Fishing was still rewarding, but these sea gulls had forgotten how to fish. For many seasons they had come to depend entirely on scraps from the nets which men from the shrimp fleets tossed to them. Finally, there were no longer any sea gulls living who knew how to fish for themselves. The shrimp boats moved on to Key West, leaving the nonproductive gulls to die in their parasitism. The first principle of life, even at the biological level, seems to be self-service. And a second principle, essential to every co-operative society that wants to be something more than sea gulls, is service of others.

We are saved as we serve. The story of J. P. Marquand's novel *Melville Goodwin, USA* is narrated by a journalist and radio commentator, Sidney, who always stands in the shadow of a general whom he once served as press agent. Deep in the story, Sidney gets one clear, frightening look at himself and his career: "It was mostly an ego-centric striving, punctuated by a few pallid efforts at escape," he pronounced. Outwardly opulent and popular, his was really a little life in a tiny moral world, cramped and pauperized. What was wrong? Sidney himself saw the trouble: "There was a gap between mediocrity and greatness which I had never crossed. . . . I had never been a self-less part of a cause. I had never tossed my life in front of me and followed it. . . . I had never commanded a lost hope. I had never obeyed a call." Marquand is too sophisticated to say it in theological language, but he is telling us that such a life characterized by "egocentric striving" is damned. Salvation does come through becoming a selfless part of a cause, through tossing our lives out in front of us and following them, through commanding lost hopes and obeying calls, which is to say that it comes through the kind of faith that is full commitment to our spiritual service.

While we are talking about election to salvation, we must hasten to insist that God never elects anyone to damnation. If God had his choice he would "have all men to be saved and to come to the knowledge of the truth." Damnation is not a failure to be elected; it is a refusal to hold office.

Notice another implication. The moral responsibility of the community rests directly upon God's elect. It is a twofold responsibility; first, to give the community a demonstration of human togetherness among the elect themselves which strikes a norm for all social groups, and second, to speak God's judgment and herald his Gospel. If a society is suffering from the disease of broken community, if it is falling into exploitation and secularism, the blame falls upon the chosen people, the church which has failed in its missions of reconciliation and redemption.

God's call comes to Christians in association with one another. It demands that they become a people and act as a saving leaven in the midst of surrounding society. As such the call is social; and this social call is primary, for Christians are meant to work in concert. But there is room also for an individual call. Presumably God has a plan for every man, enfolded in that man's peculiar nature and in the need impinging upon him, so that every man has his unique work to do and feels constrained to respond to his own individual calling. Such a man, far from being one lone individual lost in a desert waste of countless millions of men, becomes in the full sense *a man*, a man who "shall be as a hiding place from the wind, and a covert from the tempest, as streams of water in a dry place, as the shade of a great rock in a weary land."

We need greatly to return to the biblical doctrine of election. For too long we have treated the task of faith as a human elective, to be chosen or neglected from the human side, and with little consequence. It is God who elects, not men. "Ye have not chosen me, but I have chosen you, and ordained you, that ye should go and bring forth fruit, and that your fruit should remain" (A.V.). This election has staggering consequences. If we refuse to serve, the worst that can happen to the neglected world is damnation, and this can happen to us also. If

we accept, the worst that can happen to us is crucifixion
—for the world's redemption, and our own. These are
the two ways that are set before us. Whether in milder
times there may have been other ways is not for us to say
now. In this time there are only two ways, the way that
leads to destruction and the narrow, straightened way
that leads to life. There are no others.

IX ✖ *Those of the Way*

And a highway shall be there, and a way, and it shall be called The way of holiness; the unclean shall not pass over it; but it shall be for the redeemed: the wayfaring men, yea fools, shall not err therein. . . . ISAIAH 35:8

Prepare ye in the wilderness the way of the Lord; make level in the desert a highway for our God. Every valley shall be exalted, and every mountain and hill shall be made low; and the uneven shall be made level, and the rough places a plain; and the glory of the Lord shall be revealed, and all flesh shall see it together. . . . ISAIAH 40:3

(Quoted: MATTHEW 3:3; MARK 1:3; LUKE 3:4; JOHN 1:23)

But Saul . . . asked . . . for letters to . . . Damascus, so that if he found any belonging to the Way, men or women, he might bring them bound to Jerusalem. . . . ACTS 9:2

By this we may be sure that we are in him: he who says he abides in him ought to walk in the same way in which he walked.
I JOHN 2:5, 6

CHRISTIANITY is a way of life and Christians are persons who *live* in a certain distinctive manner. Early believers and their nonbelieving contemporaries took notice of this in the unique party label, *the Way*.[1] The

[1] Acts 9:2, 19:9, 23, 22:4, 24:14, 22.

term suggests that our religion is a highway and that we are travelers moving purposefully along it. In short, the label calls attention to the fact that Christianity issues in a morality, that it has its own distinguishing code of ethics.

A reading of the book of Acts leaves little doubt that *the Way* was one of the earliest designations of the new movement. The name seems at first to have been applied by the enemies of "the Nazarenes" to mark them as a sect or a heresy. Saul used it while he was caught up into the full passion of persecution. Felix and Herod Agrippa were familiar with it. The outsider, looking into the fellowship of "the Galileans," could see there a manner of life obviously different from that of any existing sect within Judaism. Features of this life which must have struck an observer were the evangelistic boldness of its adherents in proclaiming Jesus as Lord, and their communal life in familylike groups where sharing of goods was apparently without reservation. The warm solidarity of this new community of faith commanded the attention if not the tribute of the outside Jewish world, which denominated it *the Way*.

From the inside, the believers themselves looked with favor upon the name. Their minds ran quickly back to Old Testament usages which gave it dignity and significance. Jeremiah had challenged his hearers in such terms: "Behold, I set before you the way of life and the

way of death." Isaiah had sung a highway of holiness for
the redeemed: "And a highway shall be there, and a way,
and it shall be called The way of holiness; the unclean
shall not pass over it; but it shall be for the redeemed:
the wayfaring men, yea fools, shall not err therein."
These words, when repeated by the early Christian community, were part of the gospel of the realized kingdom.
They announced that the new age had dawned, that the
Lord had entered history over his great level highway
and that the faithful were following him along this boule-
vard to his coronation. Near the beginning of each of the
Four Gospels the evangelist quoted a portion of the
poetic messianic song from the fortieth chapter of Isaiah:
"The voice of one that crieth, Prepare ye in the wilderness the way of the Lord, make level in the desert a highway for our God. Every valley shall be exalted, and every
mountain and hill shall be made low; and the uneven
shall be made level, and the rough places a plain; and
the glory of the Lord shall be revealed, and all flesh shall
see it together. . . ."

That the church gathered the name to itself is seen
in the fact that it perpetuated the use of it beyond the
day of beginnings. Near the end of the first century,
writing what amounted to a long prayer addressed to
Christ in the first rather than the second person, John
called Jesus "the way, and the truth, and the life." And

about the same time, at Antioch of Syria, a Christian writing, *The Doctrina,* declared, "There are two ways in the world, that of life and that of death, of light and of darkness. Over them are set two angels, one of right, and the other of wrong."

The *way of life* in this early writing is set forth in seventy short commandments, mostly negative, preceded by a concentrated statement of Jesus' summary of the Law and the Prophets plus the Golden Rule: "The way of life is this: first, you shall love the eternal God who made you; second, your neighbor as yourself. Moreover, anything that you would not have done to you, you shall not do to anyone else." Choosing among the specific commands under this *way of life* we find these: "You shall hate nobody; some you shall love more than your own soul" (2:7). ". . . you shall not hold a grudge, or show duplicity in giving advice . . ." (2:4). "Do not be a grumbler . . ." (3:6). "Be longsuffering and upright in your business and reverent of all the words that you hear" (3:8). "You shall accept the adversities that befall you as good, knowing that nothing happens without God" (3:10). "Do not keep stretching out your hands to receive, and drawing them back when it comes to returning" (4:5).

Such are a few examples of the *way of life.* "But the way of death is the opposite of it," says *The Doctrina,* prefacing a catalogue of forty sins including adultery, murder, false witness, fornication, magic arts, enchantments, thefts, idolatry, hypocrisy, malice, covetousness, foul speech, insolence and boastfulness. The wicked who walk in the *way of death* are characterized as men "from whom gentleness is far away, and to whom boastfulness is close, seeking those who will reward them, without pity for the poor, not grieving for one who is grieved, not recognizing their creator, murderers of their sons, abortionists, turning away from good works, oppressing one who is afflicted, neglecting the appeals of the upright" (5:2).

These excerpts from *The Doctrina* show that *the Way* is a term which has come by the end of the first century to have an exclusively ethical meaning. There had been efforts to develop Christianity along nonethical lines into an aesthetic or philosophical mysticism—efforts to capture "the spirit" to the neglect of morals. Such efforts would continue for some years to come, but the main tradition of the faith was now set in the direction of ethics. Faith apart from works was declared void. There was, in fact, no aspect of Christian belief or knowledge that was not intimately tested by its fruit in a man's way of living. That hardy antagonist of heretics, the author of First John, struck a strong blow in this warfare against a nonethical Christianity: "He who says 'I know him' but disobeys his commandments is a liar, and the truth is not in him. . . . By this we may be sure that we are in him: he who says he abides in him ought to walk in the same way in which he walked."

Thus, not only have we established that *the Way* is a manner of life distinguished by its high quality of moral conduct; we have also found the norm of this conduct is the teachings and the example of Jesus of Nazareth —"his commandments" and "the way in which he walked." It remains now for us to characterize Christian morality.

To be a Christian is to regard love as the highest good and loss of love or lack of love as the greatest evil. It is to give oneself to the destruction of this evil, first in oneself, and then throughout the world. What is this love? Not sentiment, but sharing; not benevolence, but caring. To love is to discover that my life is at stake in the life of another, that his suffering is my pain, that his failure is my sin, that his waywardness is my lostness, that his recovery is my self-discovery, that his salvation is my redemption, and that his joy is my happiness. This is to love, but to love as a Christian is to be thus involved in the life of every person whom providence gives into our sphere.

This involvement of all in the life of all takes the shape of a cross, looming over the world's rim in dark silhouette against the sky. Since "all things by immortal power, near or far, hiddenly to each other linked are," no other shape shows the nature of our world nor the path of our duty so plainly. It is God's signpost pointing out the way of life. Elizabeth Cheyney in her poem, "The Man on the Cross" shows us our plain duty:

> Whenever there is silence around me
> By day or by night—
> I am startled by a cry.
> It came down from the cross—
> The first time I heard it
> I went out and searched—
> And found a man in the throes of crucifixion,
> And I said, "I will take you down,"
> And I tried to take the nails out of his feet.
> But he said, "Let them be
> For I cannot be taken down
> Until every man, every woman, and every child
> Come together to take me down."
> And I said, "But I cannot hear you cry.
> What can I do?"
> And he said, "Go about the world—
> Tell everyone you meet—
> That there is a man on the cross."

The Christian way of love involves us in living duty toward everyone we meet. The cross cannot relieve the sky of its dark shadow as long as there is yet remaining in this world one human being who has not been encircled by Christ's love.

The horizontal arms of the cross point the path of our duty, but that duty transcends obligation and soars into grateful discovery as the eye of faith follows the pointing of the vertical arm of the cross straight into the heart of God the Father. "We love, because he first loved us."

"Father" is Jesus, preferred name for God. It occurs fifteen times in the Sermon on the Mount, and it falls ⟨…⟩ance. Jesus lived con-⟨…⟩r Father's world. This ⟨…⟩ the Christian life. We ⟨…⟩ll be true sons. Let us ⟨…⟩ught that men should ⟨…⟩ He further taught that ⟨…⟩ith power.

⟨…⟩t is to be found in the ⟨…⟩ someone protests, "we ⟨…⟩wait; of what does God's ⟨…⟩on of *love*. We are far ⟨…⟩lge; we fail miserably in ⟨…⟩our lives on a personal ⟨…⟩ove for God at their cen-ters. We cannot achieve this goal, but we can approach it. Apparently, some mortals have attained it. Not possession or power, not even knowledge, is the chief goal of human life. It is nothing so individualistic, so impersonal, or so self-centered as these. It is the total personalization of life.

The author: Dwight E. Stevenson is professor of homiletics at the College of the Bible, Lexington, Kentucky, and was formerly head of the department of Bible and religion at Bethany College, Bethany, West Virginia. He has previously written *A Road Map for Sermons*, *A Guide to Expository Preaching*, and numerous study manuals for young people and adults.

It is gearing one's actions by the consideration of what they will do to persons. And this must take society into account, for no individual is a person until he stands in living relation to other selves.

To walk the way of love is to live as a member of God's family, responding to the begetting and nurturing love of God. Such belonging furnishes our social ties. We must allow no barriers of unforgiveness to separate us from our brothers. Enmity itself must be destroyed that foes may be converted into brothers. This bond also furnishes the principle of religion. Religious relationships are not legalistic or external—like those of a subject approaching a king. They are intimate and personal, like a son talking with a father, like conversation at a family table.

The righteousness of the Family of God is inward. It need not—indeed, it cannot—be legislated into being. It comes from the heart. It is voluntary, without reservations. It overflows convention and law. It springs from the inner secret of family solidarity with heartfelt respect toward all members of the family.

When love is seen as the law of life—the life of our human life—it continually beckons us to keep relations between us and others sensitively personal, free of defenses, grudges and predatory designs. Not all our life is personal. We must have some commerce with things, and to this end we must sometime temporarily use other persons as things, and we may ourselves be so used—the difference between the business function of a clerk and a vending machine is only one of versatility. But, though not all of life can be kept constantly at the personal level, all of life must be crowned there. And though persons must temporarily divest themselves of personality for concrete ends, all human beings must have a place in our hearts as persons before and after and during their commercial utility to us.

To say that this way of love involves service is to say far too little. Service can be little better than mutual exploitation. In fact, our highly impersonal society has made a great deal of "service." Let us say, rather, that the person who has discovered the extent to which he participates in the grace of receiving—from God and from his brothers —will strive to grow in the grace of giving. And he will give, not to put others in his debt and thus to gain power over them, but he will give for their sakes and for the sake of God, their Father. He will endeavor to see that his gift adds more to their beings than to their holdings.

Such is the inward dynamic of Christian behavior. In practice it does not reach this purity. Why? Because of resistance within us, the resistance of selfishness and pride, which is forever producing the illusion of our separateness and our superior importance. But there is more than this resistance from within; there is also resistance from with-

out—the resistance of highly impersonalized and imper-
sonalizing organizations and institutions through which
civilized men must act. This means that the way of love
among men in society must go forward against a backward tugging pull of individualism and collectivism,
against sin and death. This means that though love is the
law of life, it is never "successful" or easy, never entirely
"practical" in the utilitarian sense. It is the only way to
our God-given destiny as persons. It is the only way to
inward truth, through which we mount the stairs to all
cosmic Truth. By it we find our neighbors and our God,
and so come to ourselves; but it is a rugged path. The life
of love, then, becomes creative struggle against sin and
death. In a word, it is a crucifixion. The man who seeks
to save his life, even by the way of love, will lose it. Only
the man who throws his existence away for something
worthier will find his life. This is the law of love, whose
distinguishing mark is the cross.

The way of reconciliation is the way of love when the
personal fabric of life has been rent asunder. The way
of reconciliation is the path that love takes when its work
goes beyond the task of creating and conserving persons-
in-community to the merciful deed of restoring them after
they have fallen out of it.

The fabric of human community *has* been rent asunder
today. Next to the fact of impersonalization, the frag-

mentation of society is the biggest secular fact of our time. Men are living out of love—in fear, in distrust, in resentment—out of love. This is at once the cause and the nature of the divine judgment upon society in our day which we call our crisis. A German Quaker, Emil Fuchs, who has known more than his stint of suffering, sees our crisis as nothing more than a human effort to negate the indestructible fact of God's love:

How desperately people ask, "How can God be love, when all still happens that has happened in the world of men—and will go on happening in time to come?"

The same world with the same history cries out to me in a clear voice, "God is love!"

If God is love and you hate your brother, you live without God. You live without the one creative power of life. Do you wonder that you live in a world of death? Three or four thousand years ago, a poet said:

> "Thou sendest forth thy spirit; they are created:
> Thou hidest thy face, they are troubled:
> Thou takest away their breath, they die,
> And return to their dust."

When men and whole generations of men and whole nations and civilizations seek their life from wealth and power and oppression and injustice, when they live without love in greed and hate, they separate themselves from God and return to their dust.

How shall we win them back out of the dust? This brings us face to face with Christian forgiveness. William

Penn gave forgiveness a charter when he said, "Force may subdue, but love gains; and he who forgives first wins the laurel." Forgiveness, when it is Christian, has the power of reconciliation. But forgiveness is sometimes unchristian. Sometimes a man forgives out of moral snobbery, in order to feel superior to the unforgiving. Sometimes he forgives legalistically—performs a mental adjustment amounting to an impersonal erasure of a remembered wrong; he does not forgive, he merely forgets. And there is a kind of forgiveness that is nothing more than ridding oneself of the load of resentment. Undoubtedly life brings great benefits to anyone who thus foregoes revenge. If stomach ulcers are sometimes the result of resentment—or fear, which is resentment's first cousin—then physical health may be a benefit derived from this limited kind of forgiveness. Freedom from the load of hate may even release unusual creativity in a human mind, as Edwin Markham showed through days of poetic barrenness when resentment over a personal injury drove his muse from him, and as he showed again, when with resentment quenched, he sat down to receive from his returning muse one of his finest poems. The mind that is cluttered with unforgiven wrongs has little room for the inspirations of creation.

It is only when forgiveness reaches beyond the injury to the person who injured us that it becomes Christian.

Then it operates not to erase wrong but to restore fellowship. This is the depth of repentance, and its reason for being.

Markham was given spiritual penetration to see this depth of repentance. Passing beyond his injury at a wrong which a man had done, and an injustice which he had suffered, he came to see that injury as a barrier which separated him from his erstwhile brother. Then with eager hands of forgiveness he broke that barrier down:

> He drew a circle that shut me out—
> Heretic, rebel, a thing to flout.
> But Love and I had the wit to win:
> We drew a circle that took him in![2]

From the side of the fallen, love as reconciliation acts through repentance and restitution. Repentance in its essence is nothing other than a change of mind by which a person comes to see himself as a member of God's family, living voluntarily in community. He deserts his old I-center and relates himself to the New God-center. This new perspective transforms everything; most profoundly it changes him. For the first time he can see what he has done to other persons, how he has exploited them, de-

---

[2] Edwin Markham, "Outwitted," from *Poems of Edwin Markham*, selected and arranged by Charles L. Wallis (Harper, 1950). Copyright, 1950, by Virgil Markham, and used by permission of Mr. Markham.

frauded them; and he is moved with a strong compulsion to make restitution—not for the sake of righting the legal balances, but for the sake of restoring or creating fellowship. His restitution may be a deed or a word, as is fitting in its case, but its aim is to reknit the fabric of human community which had been violated. Restitution can be legalized, and any *system* of penances degrades it, but in a truly repentant life it cannot be omitted.

And to the restored, love gives a continuing commission of reconciliation. We who have been forgiven and restored to the family of God must work in the world as peacemakers. "God was in Christ reconciling the world to himself . . . and entrusting to us the message of reconciliation. So we are ambassadors for Christ, God making his appeal through us."

This is the way of life found in the Christian ethic. We are created and sustained as persons under God in the community of our acknowledged brethren. Since, through sin and impersonalism, we are always falling out of this living community and must be rescued from living death, we are redeemed and restored by forgiveness. Since our brothers continually need a like service from us, we redeem and restore them through forgiveness, which forgiveness we do not generate from ourselves but transmit from God and from the divine community in which we dwell. To receive forgiveness we must repent of our self-centeredness and our separateness. An act of restitution will then follow. After that we will find our true spiritual vocation in the ministry of reconciliation.

Such is the way of love and of reconciliation.

X ⚹ A Holy Nation

But you are a chosen race, a royal priesthood, a holy nation, God's own people, that you may declare the wonderful deeds of him who called you out of darkness into his marvelous light.
I PETER 2:9

You are the salt of the earth. . . . You are the light of the world. A city set on a hill cannot be hid. Nor do men light a lamp and put it under a bushel, but on a stand, and it gives light to all in the house. Let your light so shine before men, that they may see your good works and give glory to your Father who is in heaven. . . .   MATTHEW 5:13-16

I N THE hearts of most of us Americans these days there is a growing uneasiness about our nation. Until recently we have had an almost mystic faith in our land because we were confident that behind her vast physical resources there has always stood the massive strength of moral right-eousness. We have felt rooted in God's universe. John Fiske, a Harvard lecturer of the last century, was speaking for all of us when he bounded the United States like this:

"The United States—bounded on the north by the Aurora Borealis, on the south by the procession of the equinoxes, on the east by the primeval chaos, and on the west by the Day of Judgment." This sets our country in the heavens amid starry immensities to keep company with the truth and the goodness of God.

That was yesterday. Today we have grown uncertain. Our dollars, our gadgets, our guns do not reassure us. We are afraid that our moral foundations may be sinking from beneath us into the quicksands of compromise and corruption. Abroad, in the interest of a political balance of power, we keep company with allies like Franco whom yesterday we would have been proud to call our enemies —tyrants and dictators, we used to call them. We prop up the tottering house of Europe's decaying imperialism in the Orient, holding the wall against the growing pressure of insurgent masses of hungry and exploited peoples yearning for food and freedom. At home, an increasing number of our elected representatives govern us, not to serve us, but to dupe us and to pick our pockets. From beneath our large American cities, north and south, east and west, the octopus of the underworld reaches forth its slimy tentacles, curling them about our police, our courts, our businessmen, our congressmen, and even our athletes. With all this happening, we begin to wonder whether the United States may not be bounded not only on the west but on all sides by an encroaching Day of Judgment. Once, it may have been, we were a holy nation, but today we have shriveled to the diminutive moral stature of a Great Power.

This is an unwelcome and a disquieting conclusion, but candor compels it, or something very like it. If our plight lies in our moral deterioration, where is our moral redemption to be found? The Christian gospel finds it in the church, "a holy nation" living within the political nation. The writer of the First Letter of Peter addressed himself to the Christian community within the Roman state, when he gave them the title. "But you are a chosen race, a royal priesthood, a holy nation," he said, "God's own people, that you may declare the wonderful deeds of him who called you out of darkness into his marvelous light." He was talking about the church, not as an institution, but as a people in society living by a light that comes from above society. The seed principle of a godly nation is to be found in a people of God living within the nation.

What of the role of such a church?

As a holy nation, the church lives within the state as a people of moral integrity.

We Americans have been in the habit of assuming that moral uprightness was a native gift which comes as naturally to men as the daily sunrise. Crookedness exists, to be sure, but we are inclined to locate it in a few evil men

—demagogues, criminals, grafters—who were not molded from the same clay as we, thank heavens! This has been our most serious blunder, throwing us off guard against the sins of our own respectability. The truth is that the predatory tendency in humanity is located, not in a few men, but in all of us. Our moral uprightness is not so much like the daily rising of the sun, as it is like toiling with the sweat of our brows and the ache of our backs in a garden which the weeds will take as soon as we neglect it. Morality was defined by the psychologist William James at the turn of the century as *"action in the line of greatest resistance."* "The ideal impulse," he said, "appears [as] . . . a still small voice which must be artificially reinforced to prevail."

Christians know this. All of us feel the downward dragging pull of our own love of comfort, our moral inertia, our selfishness, our pigheaded prejudice and our anxiety. Sin is no abstraction to us; it is a daily antagonist. Most of us know that temptation would hold us helpless in its iron grasp, were not the ideal impulse within us reinforced by our awareness of Christian companions who march shoulder to shoulder with us in the strife, and by our communion with God who stands within the shadows, keeping watch above his own.

There is, in fact, only one kind of insurance against temptation. This is the frank acknowledgment that since every man has his price, the only way we can guard against selling out to compromise is to sell out to God. We are bribeproof insofar as we have already sold ourselves to God. And this we have done if we are Christians, for then we are "a holy nation, God's own people." Peter Marshall, that late genius who served so notably as chaplain of the United States Senate, once led the Upper House of Congress in this prayer: "O God, help us to stand for something, lest we fall for anything." That is the price of our immunity to corruption.

In the same way, John Calvin of Geneva drove straight to the secret of moral integrity four hundred years ago when he wrote:

> We are not our own; therefore let us not presuppose it as our end to seek what may be expedient for us according to the flesh. . . .
> On the contrary, we are God's; to him, therefore, let us live and die.
> We are God's; therefore let his wisdom and will preside in all our actions.
> We are God's; towards him, therefore, as our only legitimate end, let every part of our lives be directed.[1]

There, then, lies our integrity—not in our straining effort to be captains of our own souls, but in our complete surrender to the will and the power of God, possessing us. Christians are "God's own people" who constitute a holy

---

[1] John Calvin, *Institutes of the Christian Religion*, Bk. III, ch. 7, 1.

nation living within the state as a people of moral integrity.

As a holy nation, the church is a people acting as a saving power within the state.

Jesus, speaking to the earliest community of disciples, drew their attention to this redemptive mission: "You are the salt of the earth. . . . You are the light of the world." Both of these figures denote a moral force. Salt saves food from flatness and from decay; light banishes darkness. Christians, then, are in the world to season and save it from moral flatness and rottenness, and to shine in the darkness banishing the night of wrong.

Such figures of speech strike directly at our desire to practice our religion as a thing apart from our common ventures of life in secular society. We Protestants do not, of course, believe in monasticism; we say that we do not condone leaving the world and going into a cloister to be religious. But may we not be guilty of a kind of Protestant monasticism, nevertheless? Our church building becomes our monastery, behind whose walls we repair to be religious. The Sunday gathering is not our power-house from which our life lines run out into the secular world to give it moral light and power; it is our bushel under which we hide our light from the secular world. Christians who do nothing more than gather in corporate worship and study for their own mutual edification on Sundays are lights under Gothic bushels.

God expects his church as a holy nation to be something more than this. Speaking through the great unknown prophet of the Exile to ancient Israel, God said, "Thou art my servant; Israel, in whom I will be glorified. . . . It is too light a thing that thou shouldest be my servant to raise up the tribes of Jacob, and to restore the preserved of Israel: [That is, it is not worthy of you to do nothing more than restore the preserved of Israel.] I will also give thee for a light to the Gentiles, that thou mayest be my salvation unto the end of the earth." Paraphrase this, bring it down to date, and apply it to God's new Israel, his holy nation the church: "Thou art my servant, O Church of God, in whom I will be glorified. It is too light a thing that thou shouldest be my servant only among Presbyterians, Methodists and Disciples; I will also give thee for a light to those outside the church, that thou mayest be my salvation throughout secular society."

If Christians are to act redemptively, they must live as Christians beyond the church. Christians are salt, and light, and leaven; but the salt must be in the food, the light must shine in the darkness, and the leaven must be yeast in the meal.

If the church as a holy nation cannot withdraw from secular society behind its own walls to practice its religion, neither can it operate purely as a political pressure group. There will be times—no doubt ours is one of them—when Christians will have to throw themselves into reform movements, coercing a corrupt society to yield up a fuller measure of decency; but such movements are stopgaps. To rely solely upon them is to heal the hurt of the people lightly. Something far more searching and demanding is required of us.

Congressman Walter P. Judd of Minnesota, speaking to two thousand Disciple laymen at the Campbell Home Retreat at Bethany, West Virginia, said that it is a species of moral stupidity to let political machines elect corrupt politicians and then rain a deluge of letters upon them in the hopes of forcing them to become noble overnight and behave like statesmen. We need intelligent, informed and dedicated Christian men who will be concerned enough to *get into politics* as their divine calling. More than we need Christians standing outside political circles pointing the finger of shame at politicians, we need Christians among the politicians.

We are just as blameworthy when we allow industry and big business to grow up in a pagan soil, and then organize church pressure groups, pass convention resolutions, and preach sermons, thus hoping to compel a pagan tree rooted in secular soil to produce the Christian fruits of justice and mercy. We must have Christians who will go into business and industry by way of an ordination to the Christian ministry within business and industry.

A holy nation of Christians living by moral principles in their vocations in the midst of civil society can save that society. More than 55 per cent of our American population belongs to churches. Taking this percentage as a general basis, think of the potential moral force that Christians could exert from within the various trades and professions! There are, for example, 147,565 medical doctors in the American Medical Association. Presumably 70,000 or 75,000 of them, at least, are Christians—a body of doctors strong enough to do something revolutionary about the unmet medical needs of our backward areas. There are nearly half a million public school teachers; half of these—even a fifth of them—could capture the mind of our children and youth for righteousness, if they considered their vocation religiously. The Christians among 90,000 engineers could make a resounding moral impact upon industry; and 75,000 Christian lawyers could certainly take long strides toward cleaning up the courts of America. If the other professions got to working at this job, perhaps something could even be done about America's 150,000 clergymen; half of them might become Christian enough to instill the mind of Christ into the churches.

We need not go further. You know that if there is gambling in your city, if there is corruption in the police,

in the courts, and graft in business, it is because a luxur-
iant underworld has its roots in the fertile soil of respectable society. That respectable society is made up in large
part of bankers and merchants, doctors and lawyers,
mechanics and secretaries who are not now working at
the Christian calling within their vocations. If it should
happen tomorrow that every citizen of your town who was
in church last Sunday should enter his place of employ-
ment as a committed Christian, there is no morally de-
sirable change in the life of your city that could not be
brought to pass within six months.

The power of Christians from within the trades and
professions could be explosive and transforming, if we
could begin to think of ourselves as God's own people, a
holy nation with a divine mission of the job. Tertullian, a
church father who lived about A.D. 200, once said to his
Roman neighbors, "We [Christians] are of yesterday. Yet
we have filled everything of yours, cities, tenements, for-
tresses, towns, markets, the very camps, divisions, companies, palace, senate, forum. We have left you only the
temples. . . . We could, both unarmed and without insur-
rection, join battle with you by just going on strike."
If Tertullian could claim such power for the Christian
movement near its dawn when its numbers were small,
what would he say of it now in America, with a constitu-
ency of nearly eighty million members?

It only remains for us to think of ourselves all through

the week as members of the church in the midst of the world, committed to the Christian ministry through our vocations. If large numbers of Christians, thinking of themselves as a holy nation within the political nation, were to begin doing this, what would their action involve? Perhaps we can illustrate. Suppose you are a lawyer. If you really want to take your Christian citizenship seriously, you may find yourself very quickly doing at least three things:

First, you will go to your office tomorrow morning as a Christian who has been called to the ministry of men and of God through the profession of law. You will approach your work in a religious frame of mind, as a member—a hand or a foot or a tongue—of the body of Christ, responsive to the mind of Christ. You will undertake your job as a spiritual service.

Second, you will not think of yourself like Elijah under the juniper tree alone and hounded in your moral integrity. You will remember the seventy-five thousand other Christian lawyers who may not have bowed the knee to Baal. They are in their offices today. Think of what a moral force your united witness could be in the courts of the land in this one day!

Third, if you have come this far, you will want to take at least one more step. You will want to consult with some of these fellow Christians who are also striving to serve

God through the profession of law. You may even want
to create a small group of ten or twelve of your fellows
who will meet more or less regularly across the next weeks
and months to conduct serious and detailed research into
the question, "Just what does it mean to practice law as
a Christian in this city when facing the issues that we face
here today and tomorrow and this week?" Such a vocational research group need by no means confine its membership within the denominations. It need not even be
narrowed to Protestants. For all the doctrinal, liturgical
and ecclesiastical divergences within our religion, there
is a remarkable community of moral and ethical agreement. Christian lawyers of different religious bodies have
far more in common than they have with their non-Christian fellow lawyers. A research fellowship of the sort
described ought to be a hard-working, fact-finding group
which is not afraid of candor and criticism. It ought also
to meet in an atmosphere of prayer.

What has been said about the legal profession could be
a working program for every vocational group in your
city, and throughout the nation. Who is willing to take
the proposal seriously? Do you really want a Christian
nation? Are you concerned enough, not only to belong to
the church and to go to church, but to *be* the church in
the world—"a holy nation, God's own people"? That is
what God wants of you. He has summoned you "that you

may declare the wonderful deeds of him who called you out of darkness into his marvelous light."

The church, when considered not as a fellowship of Christians meeting together, but as a solidarity of people who are scattered like salt and leaven through society, is a holy nation within the political nation. As such, it lives in integrity by a moral law from above the state, and it exerts a transforming moral influence upon the state. But this is not the end of the matter. This holy nation of which we Christians are citizens has an international mission also.

As a holy nation, the church is lodged in the body of all nations, and, living by a sovereignty above them all, is the spiritual soul that holds them together.

We are only now beginning to recapture the world-wide solidarity of the church universal which the early Christians of Roman times knew to be so real. We are beginning to create the instruments of international consultation and communication through the ecumenical movement. There is a growing determination to overcome our agelong fragmentation of the one body of Christ into a multitude of severed national and denominational organs of that body. Bishop Brent's "Call to Unity" issued at Lausanne finds an echo in all our hearts: "God has used, beyond anything we had a right to expect, our divided Christendom. But now that we know the sin and

disaster of sectarianism, we cannot hope He will use it
much longer. . . . It is He that will change us . . . the
impossible into the possible, and bring about the con-
summation of Christian hope in a Church that will be one
flock under one shepherd." That Lausanne call, issued
in 1927, sounded in the midst of what has proved since to
be a growing shout for a world-wide Christian community. Voices lifted then have increased in volume and
in convicting power until it is possible for a church historian to give it as his sober judgment that in the years
between 1914 and 1948, "Christians were being knit
more consciously into a world-wide fellowship than had
been the case since the first three centuries when the
Catholic Church was coming into being."

A great new horizontal fellowship carries across national boundaries, uniting peoples of all races, nations
and cultures into a living whole. We are now beginning
to think of ourselves as *ecumenical*. The ancestry of this
word is revealing. The Greek word *oikos, house,* developed into *oikoumene,* the *world-house* or the *whole in-
habited earth.* The adjective *ecumenical* means *universal*;
but the picture it gives us is full of imagination: It shows
us the world as a home, housing the whole human family.

As the ecumenical church, operating through the
world-wide loyalties of each of us, comes into its own, it
will begin again to dissolve man-made barriers. What it

once did to the cultural barrier between Jews and Greeks, it will do again to political and social walls and curtains: "For he is our peace, who has made us both one, and has broken down the dividing wall of hostility . . . that he might create in himself one new man [humanity] in place of two, so making peace, and might reconcile us both to God in one body through the cross, thereby bringing the hostility to an end."

That all of this does something radical to old-line patriotism is immediately clear. No American Christian these days can draw a circle that shuts the Russian Christian out—and some Russian Christians are also communists! We do not have a united pacifist witness, and we do not even know that God intends us to have such a witness, but we do feel a community of concern with every serious Christian across every hostile military barrier in our world, and we are finding ways of expressing that community even through the anomaly of conflict. Whatever World War II may have done, it did not shatter the unity of the church; rather the church emerged from it more completely one than at any time in this century, or in many centuries.

Obviously, such a horizontal fellowship would be impossible without a transcendent loyalty which lifts our allegiance above every state to the sovereign rule of God within the nations and over the nations. And it is this loyalty to God and his righteous will which can supply the community of moral consent which must be the core of all international law and all world government. Visiting at Lake Success in the headquarters of the United Nations just before Christmas in 1949, a group of ministers and educators heard the officers of that great body refer again and again to "moral force." They emphasized that the United Nations had no other power with which to achieve its ultimate purpose, and they admitted that they could not themselves generate that moral force; they could only use what had been and was being generated by the faith of the world's peoples in a cosmic moral order. This is where the church as a holy nation plays its vital role.

While nation-bound men chant the death song of narrow patriotism, "We have no king but Caesar," Christians lift their voices in a ringing oratorio to the "King of Kings and Lord of Lords." They live and serve in the faith that "the kingdom of the world has become the kingdom of our Lord and of his Christ, and he shall reign for ever and ever."

An unknown Christian writer of the early centuries wrote a letter known as . . . "The Address to Diognetus." In it we find this theme—the unity of the world through a holy nation within the nations which pays homage to a sovereign and a law above all the nations. He wrote:

Christians are not distinguished from the rest of mankind in country or speech or customs. For they do not live somewhere in cities of their own or use some distinctive language . . . [yet] their own way of life which they display is wonderful and admittedly strange. They live in their native lands, but like foreigners. They take part in everything like citizens, and endure everything like aliens. Every foreign country is their native land, and every native land a foreign country. . . . They remain on earth, but they are citizens of heaven. They obey the established laws, and in their own lives they surpass the laws. . . . To put it briefly, what the soul is to the body, Christians are to the world. The soul is scattered through all parts of the body, and Christians are, through all the cities of the world. The soul lives in the body but it is not of the body; Christians also live in the world, but they are not of the world. . . . The soul is shut up in the body, but itself holds the body together; and Christians are kept in the world . . . but themselves hold the world together.

As long as there is this holy nation spread throughout all nations, political states may not without bad conscience relax the right and succumb to might. They may not forsake the pursuit of international understanding and cooperation, however tempting it may be to withdraw from the United Nations and "go it alone." The claims of worldwide justice for all citizens of all states will not be silenced in the ears of rulers; and the cry of war-weary millions to be quit of carnage will rise and swell until it is answered.

For the voice of the universal church will get through to some statesmen, like President Eisenhower, who will then give words to its call, as he did in the spring of 1953 before the American Society of Newspaper Editors:

Every gun that is made, every warship launched, every rocket fired signifies—in the final sense—a theft from those who hunger and are not fed, those who are cold and are not clothed. . . .

The cost of one modern heavy bomber is this: a modern brick school in more than 30 cities.

It is: two electric power plants, each serving a town of 60,000 population.

It is: two fine, fully equipped hospitals.

It is some 50 miles of concrete highway.

We pay for a single fighter plane with a half-million bushels of wheat.

We pay for a single destroyer with new homes that could have housed more than 8,000 people. . . .

This is not a way of life at all, in any true sense.

We could not long contemplate the global scene without becoming sensitive to the role of the church in melting racial barriers. The peoples of the world are, in the majority, colored peoples. In our own America, one person in ten is colored. Millions of these brown, black, red, yellow sons of our Father are also our Christian "brothers under the skin." White prejudice, once complacently snobbish and secure, is retreating in disorder today before the moral pressure of a Christianity which has been channeled into Western society through the church, and which, ironically, has sometimes been taken more seriously by labor unions and by secular colleges than by

Christian institutions. Perhaps we need to paraphrase one of George Bernard Shaw's celebrated sayings: "An upsurge of Christian conscience is arising. Its force is so great that not even the Christian church will be able to resist it."

For nearly fifty years we have been singing a hymn whose prophetic meanings are working their way into our blood—"In Christ there is no East or West. . . ." The words of the third stanza would surely choke in the throat of any white Christian who still clings to his pagan notions of his own racial superiority:

> Join hands then, Brothers of the Faith,
> Whate'er your race may be!—
> Who serves my Father as a son
> Is surely kin to me.

The implications of citizenship in this supranational society, the church as a holy nation within the nations, are demanding. If one takes them seriously, he may feel compelled to do some of the following things:

First, he will reach toward his fellow Christians in all lands daily with hands of prayer. His local church will never be a lone, isolated "little house in this mean street" of provincial concern. It will be a cosmic communications center in touch with God and his whole world. Every Lord's Supper will be for him a world-wide communion; every private and corporate act of worship, a world fellowship of prayer.

Second, he will contribute generously to the world mission as his mission, which he discharges either directly or through his gifts. He will act upon the belief that there can be no genuinely local church; if it is local it cannot be Christian; if it is Christian it will not be local.

Third, he will lend his support, and, if occasion permits, his presence, to the great ecumenical conferences of the church. He will support the ecumenical movement abroad and in his own community, always seeking aggressively to enlarge the sphere of Christian co-operation. He will be, in short, a Christian internationalist.

Fourth, he will individually discharge toward the human beings who make up his face-to-face world of persons the obligations of Christian brotherliness. On the job, on street and streetcar, in school and home and church, he will be living upon a plane of higher citizenship and within a sphere of more inclusive human community. Whatever social reforms he may induce society to enact for the future, his own personal reform will have been passed and ratified in his own life; he will be living daily as neighbor and as brother to those concrete persons, of whatever race, with whom it is his lot to deal. Over all the earth it may be true that "the kingdom tarries long," but in his own small world of actual persons met daily in the flesh, as far as he is able to will and to do it, he will "bring in the day of brotherhood, and end the night of wrong." For him, God's kingdom will have come.

Have you been despairing of your nation and of the world in which America is a leading power? Then despair no longer. The horizon of your hopes is not limited by political boundaries. If you are a Christian you belong also to another nation, a holy nation, which has a heroic, urgent mission to perform in saving this nation and in leading the way out of international anarchy toward a great new commonwealth of nations. Take up the duties of this higher citizenship courageously and believingly. You can begin where you are, today.

XI ✳ Members of the Body of Christ

Now you are the body of Christ and individually members of it. . . . I CORINTHIANS 12:27

For as in one body we have many members, and all the members do not have the same function, so we, though many, are one body in Christ, and individually members one of another. . . .
ROMANS 12:4, 5

TODAY'S secular world is a society of tired individualists who are trying to lose themselves in the human mass. Priding themselves on their independence of other persons, typical moderns actually have neither the courageous conviction nor the moral inclination to stand apart from the crowd. Our Constitution grants us freedom of speech, but we have few independent judgments that we want to talk about, and few causes that are uniquely ours. Increasingly the average man has no voice that is not an echo of other voices, no opinions but those marketed by the newspaper and the newscast, no tastes but those of the billboards, the magazine advertisement and the radio commercial. It is of such stuff that slave states are made.

How did he arrive at this anomaly—rugged individual sunk in the mire of mass-mindedness? Largely through clutching at the freedom of privilege while rejecting the freedom of responsibility; he wanted to be free from men in spite of the fact that he is so constituted that he can be free only when he is among them. Complete separation from society, being a warping of human nature from its norm (which norm is individuality-in-community), springs back toward an opposite extreme of absolute submersion under society.

If we are to be saved from this malady, we shall have to recapture the Christian understanding of the *person*, who is both an individual and at the same time a responsible member of society. And this, after all, is precisely what our Christian faith does when it is allowed to operate from its own genius; for to be a Christian, in Paul's instructive figure, is to be a member of the body of Christ. This figure, so often examined to determine the nature of the church, will repay study in order to determine the nature of the Christian.

As members of the body of Christ, Christians are different from one another, as hands and feet are different, or eyes and ears. Each has his unique capacities which are

God-given and which call him to the self-respecting service which he alone can render to God and humanity. In
the Christian society there is room—even a demand—
for individualism.

The Christian movement began with a core of leaders
who were ruggedly individualistic. What a heterogeneous
group the twelve disciples were. Here, at the very spear-
head of our history, says Dr. William Robinson, we find
a band made up of "a 'collaborator' and an extreme
nationalist, together with one who approximated an
anarchist; of fishermen; of the well-to-do owner class and
of the workman class; of a scientific-minded unbeliever
like Thomas and of a guileless innocent like Nathanael."
And in the earliest church, how different was Paul from
James the Brother of Jesus, and Peter from John.

To expand the circle, consider the Pentecostal crowd
from whom Christianity won its earliest converts. Hear
Luke tell it: There came together on this birthday of the
church "devout men from every nation under heaven . . .
Galileans . . . Parthians and Medes and Elamites and
residents of Mesopotamia, Judea and Cappadocia, Pontus
and Asia, Phrygia and Pamphylia, Egypt and the parts of
Lybia belonging to Cyrene, and visitors from Rome, both
Jews and proselytes." Think of the cultural contrasts, the
linguistic differences, the racial varieties. This is a good
lesson for a white, Anglo-Saxon, middle-class congrega-

tion to ponder. When Paul called the roll of his church, he found no such colorless uniformity; his census included Greek and Jew, circumcized and uncircumsized, barbarian, Scythian, slave, free man . . . male and female, rich and poor, noble and low-born, learned and unschooled.

There were other differences in that early church. Antioch did not organize the fellowship as Jerusalem had done, nor did Galatia follow the lead of either in its organizational structure. Worship also differed. Christians at Jerusalem continued to meet in the temple; Corinthian Christians meticulously abstained from all contact with the cultus of their pre-Christian faiths.

The whole picture that we get of the early church is one boldly emphasizing "varieties of gifts . . . varieties of service . . . and varieties of working." There was room within that primitive fellowship for wide individual and group differences. What then must we infer about Christians today? That they too should be expected to differ, and that each one, as a member of a believing community, should be encouraged to be uniquely himself.

But let us not be misled. We derive the right and the mandate to be different not from our individual separateness, but from our *belonging*. It is only through the experience of membership that we can withstand the otherwise overwhelming impulse to be like everybody else.

When we think of ourselves as a part of a larger whole, we gain courage to be ourselves; we do not need to ape anyone. But when we think of ourselves as separate, we must try to be everybody at once. We cannot bear it that anyone has or can do anything that we are debarred from. Thus in separateness we lose our identity, but in membership we find it. "For the body does not consist of one member but of many."

Christian individualism is rooted in Christian community. Paul saw this. "If the foot should say, 'Because I am not a hand, I do not belong to the body,' that would not make it any less a part of the body." Of course, no foot conscious of the fact that it was a part of a body would want to be a hand; only a foot thinking of itself and of the hand as separate and independent of a body would try to imitate the hand.

And Paul never confused unity with uniformity. Genuine organic unity encourages and thrives upon individual differences. It does not press persons into one mold. "If the whole body were an eye, where would be the hearing? If the whole body were an ear, where would be the sense of smell? But as it is, God arranged the organs in the body, each one of them, as he chose. If all were a single organ, where would the body be? As it is, there are many parts, yet one body." This is such a familiar scripture that we sometimes fail to see the absurdity that Paul has here painted so humorously. Suppose, he said, that persons, despising their God-given uniqueness as members of God-given community, try to imitate others, what would be the result? It would be like a human body that had turned into one huge, glaring eye, or into one enormous ear to out-elephant all elephants' ears! But such a disconnected eye or ear would be a dead monstrosity, nothing more. Human uniformity is mechanical, not living; it derives from a horde of separated and "independent" individuals. Human unity is alive, and it is created by persons who voluntarily become members of a spiritual community. Christian individualism is rooted in Christian community.

What is Christian individualism? It is the self-respect that comes from knowing oneself to be a part of God's design, a member of a strong human community which is rooted in the intention of God. It is uniqueness put to work in the service of those who need what we can do. It is developing into one's own latent capacities for the glory of God. It is integrity that refuses to budge from a position assigned by conscience. It is not privilege, nor is it license; but it is liberty, the liberty of the sons of God.

Horace Bushnell was drawing upon just such Christian individualism when, in his celebrated sermon "Every

Man's Life a Plan of God," he said to his Hartford congregation:

Ten, twenty, fifty, seventy years ago, you came into this living world, and began to breathe this mortal air. The guardian angel that came to take charge of you said, "To this end is he born, for this cause is he come into the world." God . . . had a definite plan for you, a good end settled and cherished for you in his heart. This it was that gave meaning and glory to your life. Apart from this, it was not, in his view, life for you to live; it was accident, frustration, death. What now, O soul, hast thou done? What progress hast thou made? How much of the blessed life-plan of thy Father hast thou executed? How far on thy way art thou to the good, best end thy God has designed for thee?

We are individuals, but if we are Christians we are together as voluntary members of a community. We are organically dependent upon one another; we accept that fact and find our freedom within it.

It is not Christians alone who are connected to one another. All human beings are organically bound to other human beings. This is the structure of our human nature. Each person lives as a human being in constant interaction with the ideas, the wishes, the needs, the demands and the services of other persons. In this living network he both receives and gives, he molds and is molded. We have dramatic proof of this every time transportation becomes snowbound and a city is denied incoming foodstuffs, every time our son imitates a playmate, every time an infant speaks the first words of his mother tongue, every time we acquire knowledge from another or use an invention sprung from some human mind, and every time we nourish our spirits at the springs of friendship. We are so deeply immersed in the sea of human community that we are scarcely aware of its existence, but like the fish in the sea, we would soon die as human beings if we were lifted out of it.

Some men live blindly in this human interdependence. They draw upon it for their life, but they do not knowingly contribute to it. Others live rebelliously, in self-frustrating denial of the existence of such interdependence. They deny the very nature of their human nature. They live against themselves. They do not succeed in destroying their dependence upon other human beings but only in distorting genuine human community into parasitism, fadism, mass-mindedness and political regimentation. They are the pagan individualists of our time.

The absurdity of denying our interdependence is classically set forth in the myth of creation from the ancient Greek philosopher Empedocles. In the primeval state of existence, he averred, "many heads sprung up without necks, and arms wandered here and there bereft of shoulders. Eyes strayed up and down in want of foreheads. Solitary limbs wandered seeking union." Such separated existences of organs meant to be together being intolerable, "these things joined themselves together as each might chance, and many other things arose. Shambling creatures with faces and breasts looking in different direction were born; some offspring of oxen with the faces of men, others . . . offspring of men with the heads of oxen. . . ." How fittingly these mythical monsters symbolize the unnatural communities which frustrated hyperindividualists are compelled to build up!

Christians are neither unknowing nor rebellious participants in human community. They are knowing, willing and contributing members of it. This means that, like the New Testament, we know nothing of a separated, individual Christian. There may be men who remain morally upright without holding membership in an institutional church, but nobody who stands alone is a Christian. We must bear one another's burdens if we would fulfill the law of Christ. "If one member suffers, all suffer together; if one member is honored, all rejoice together." It is not our goodness that makes us Christians, but the quality of our togetherness.

It is important to notice that Christian togetherness is never collectivism; it is checked at every instant by Christian individualism. This being true, Christian togetherness is a harmony of differences. William Robinson, in a continuation of the quotation already taken from *The Biblical Doctrine of the Church*, makes this harmony abundantly clear as he discusses the fellowship of the Twelve:

> Here was the church in embryo, and it was a typical church at that. This is what fellowship means, not the gathering together of a group of like-minded uninteresting people calculated to bore anyone other than themselves, but the nonexplosive interlocking of those rich differences of personality which, if left to themselves or organized on a class basis, would lead to endless strife.

Here, then, is the Christian insurance against both pagan individualism that runs riot and pagan collectivism which devours jaded individualists. It is found in the Christian community of persons. "For just as the body is one and has many members, and all the members of the body, though many, are one body, so it is with Christ."

There is, however, one more important thing that must be said about being members of the body of Christ. It is that the body as an organism and we as its organs come into being, live and act in response to the spirit of Christ. All men are spiritual beings seeking their life in a faith and their membership in a community which holds together through that faith. For Christians these requirements are fulfilled in Christ.

To say that the church is the body of Christ is, of course, to say that it is the physical agency through which Christ does his work in the world of time. In that sense,

Christ is dependent upon his church; but we must be very sure that we are talking about the *church* and not about some institutional deposit of the church of another age or some deceptive substitute for the church. The Corpus Christi, it has been observed, can easily become the corpse of Christ! The body can live on without the spirit, in which case it has ceased to be the body of Christ and has degenerated into one of the numerous bodies of humanity. The church must have its forms—organization, cultus, clergy, property—but it cannot derive its life from them. It, as an organism, and we, as organs, derive *life* from Christ himself.

If the church is the body of Christ, *Christ creates it.* He creates it, a soul fashioning a body, by calling "new creatures" to be its members. He creates it in faith and grace. Men who respond to his call put off the I-center and cleave to the Christ-center. They are new in their relationships, new in their values, new in their motivations and their goals. From division against themselves, from aimlessness, from spiritual isolation, from un-brotherliness and hopelessness they are saved "out of death into life," and they become individually members of Christ, and collectively the church of Christ.

This means, of course, that no merely formal joining of a church makes a Christian. It means that many supposed members of churches are not members of the true body of

Christ. It means that some supposed "outsiders" are included. And it means that the institution of the church must always serve as an instrument for bringing persons individually into full communion with the saving Christ. Persons cannot "*join* the church." They can only be born as new creatures in Christ who thereby *become* the church.

Moreover, if the church is the body of Christ, *Christ animates it*. His spirit lives in it and in its members, and that spirit gives the members their vitality, their nourishment and their renewal. From the human side, this is to say that serving Christ becomes the ruling passion of our lives. History is far from lacking in men who could have said with Paul, "For me to live is Christ." Even contemporary history has many inspiring examples of lives controlled completely by the spirit of Christ; but the quality of their passion and our urgent need of it now are best illustrated by reading part of a letter from a young Chinese, twenty-one years of age, who, though reared and educated in a Christian mission, has now become a zealous Communist. He writes:

Now I am no longer the former man you knew. Apart from my body which is the same, my whole mind and thought have changed. I have become a new man in a classless revolution pioneer corps, a loyal believer of Marx-Leninism. I shall never live for myself alone but for the masses. What satisfies my aspirations now is the progress of a happy socialism to a communist state.

In this new teaching I have found unimagined blessing and happiness. I am very sorry that I must inform you that I no longer believe in God nor worship him. I can no longer address you as a religious brother, but I send you my revolutionary love.[1]

Surely he has taken a leaf out of the Christian book!

Christians too must be able to say, "Apart from my body which is the same, my whole mind and thought have changed. . . . I shall never live for myself alone. . . . I send you my revolutionary love." If Christians, so called, do not learn how to say this from the heart, the world will be captured by those who can.

Finally, if we are members of the body of Christ, *Christ activates us*. We move, like his hands and feet, in obedience to his will. And we make no move that is not prompted by him. This introduces all our life into Christ, who "is all, and in all." He is present when we sit in our houses, and when we walk by the way, and when we lie down and when we rise up. He is among the pots and pans in the kitchen, among the books in the schoolroom, at the cash register in our business, at the ballot box and the legislator's desk in politics. For we act at all these places in our conscious capacity of being the hands of Christ or his feet, the eyes or ears of Christ, or his lips speaking his Word of Life.

We began this chapter with a tired individualist trying

[1] Elton Trueblood, "The Christian Counter-Revolution," *The Pulpit*, Feb., 1952.

to lose himself in the mass of humanity. At one point at least his instinct is correct—his desire to lose himself in something bigger than he is. But if his losing is also to be a finding, it must not be in the mass of humanity. It must be in Christ. Then will he find himself again through finding his brother, and his God. And thus will he come into his full humanity—a person vitally sustained in spiritual community.

XII ✻ *Aliens and Exiles*

Beloved, I beseech you as aliens and exiles to abstain from the passions of the flesh that wage war against your soul. . . .

I PETER 2:11

Do not love the world or the things in the world. If any one loves the world, love for the Father is not in him. For all that is in the world, the lust of the flesh and the lust of the eyes and the pride of life, is not of the Father but is of the world. And the world passes away, and the lust of it; but he who does the will of God abides for ever. . . . I JOHN 2:15-17

But our commonwealth is in heaven, and from it we await a Savior, the Lord Jesus Christ. . . . PHILIPPIANS 3:20

MODERN man feels himself to be a prisoner of time, shut up in the burning house of a perishing civilization. He finds himself incapable of arresting the blaze; on the contrary, every action he takes seems but to fan the fire and hasten the final dissolution of the house into the ashes of its doom. Who is this victim? He is the man who proclaimed himself master of time, planner and propagator of civilization. Whence comes this modern version of hell? It comes from the attempt to make this world man's heaven, to transmute values into things, to squeeze eternity into a mortal lifetime. This death is happening to the very man who affirmed, "I love life, and I want to live!" This misery comes to the one who wistfully sings, "I want to be happy, and I want you to be happy too." Such is the paradox of this-worldiness. Those most at home in time are most threatened by it. Those most completely naturalized as citizens of civilization are most violently repudiated by it. Those clinging most tenaciously to life are most paralyzed by death.

From the Christian point of view, the rescue of modern man, the time-trapped animal, lies in a recovery of the sense of transcendence. Man, according to the Gospel, lives in this world but is never destined to be a fully naturalized citizen of this world. His citizenship is elsewhere, in eternity. He moves in time, in a political state, in a culture and a civilization as a participant who is also an alien and an exile—a stranger and a pilgrim. The Christian, that is to say, has one foot planted very firmly on the earth, but he has the other foot in heaven.

And now the Christian paradox begins to work. Accepting physical death as a fact, but not as a meaning, he is uncowed by force or by threat of death, and lives life to the full. Values now become more real to him than happiness; thus he comes to his integrity, the source of enduring happiness. Possessing things never comes first with him; therefore he is never enslaved by them, but truly possesses them. Civilization is no god to him, but because he lives in the soul of culture—in a faith—he is the creator and savior of civilizations. In the state he lives above the law, but his conscience is the source of law. His mortal life, dwarfed by eternity, becomes a brief sojourn; but for that very reason his every moment comes to him trailing clouds of immortal glory. The most satisfactory life on this earth, the most victorious use of mortality, the most creative citizenship depend ultimately upon those whose "commonwealth is in heaven."

This citizenship in an eternal world gives the Christian a saving sense of detachment from pagan society. It provides him, as it were, with a platform from which he can look upon his social world critically, discerning its imperfections.

There are, of course, various non-Christian forms of detachment which must be rejected here. Extreme otherworldliness, for example, consigns this material world to Satan and projects human concerns entirely beyond it to a "golden strand" in "the sweet bye-and-bye." The result, one suspects, is that the devotees of such a faith do not live in this world while they are in it, and find themselves unprepared to live in the next world when they arrive at it. But, worse still, believers of this persuasion abandon God's children on this earth to injustices and inhumanities of the most hellish kind, minimizing the evil of these cruelties by pious platitudes about a world where ultimately there will be "not a tear, not a sigh." Extreme otherworldliness of this sort ignores the doctrine of Creation; God made the world, and "he saw that it was good." This world may not be the whole of God's universal dominion, but it is a part of it; as such it is real and holy. Mortal time cannot be equated with eternity, but it is assuredly embraced and contained in eternity; a part of it is not apart from it. We must reject the detachment of extreme otherworldliness.

Likewise, and for much the same reasons, we must reject the detachment of monasticism. Christian withdrawal is not a physical separation from society; it is a moral and spiritual withdrawal from the pagan attitudes and practices of secular society. "I beseech you as aliens and exiles," said the Apostolic writer, "to abstain from the passions of the flesh that wage war against your soul." Christians are to live in pagan society. They are to be different but not separate. Else they will not be the leaven working in the meal or the light shining in the darkness. We must reject the detachment of monasticism as well as that of extreme otherworldliness.

In the same way, we must reject the detachment of the aesthetic bystander who does not participate in this world's struggles but who looks on them with the huge pleasure of one who enjoys the spectacle. Philosopher George Santayana is such a bystander—confessedly so. "I like to be a stranger myself—it was my destiny," he recently wrote in his autobiography. What is more, he said, "I wish to be the only stranger. For this reason I have been happiest among people of all nationalities who were not of my own age, class, or family circle; for then I was a single exceptional personage in their world, and they a completely harmonious milieu for me to drop into and live with for a season."[1] Santayana likes to be a spectator, but he wants to be the only one; he does not like to associate with large numbers of other spectators, or to be thrown into a society composed of them. Thus he reveals the anomaly of his detachment; it is at bottom a parasitic attachment to an orderly, going society from which he draws not only his food and drink (by way of financial inheritance) but also his aesthetic enjoyment.

The Christian, as alien and exile, lives a detached life in the midst of pagan society but his is not a detachment like any of the three we have just examined. He is no ghostly shade haunting the world of flesh and blood and he is no spectator. It is from the paganism of pagan society that he is detached.

[1] George Santayana, "I Like to Be a Stranger," *The Atlantic Monthly*, May, 1952.

That paganism was never more profoundly epitomized than in the First Letter of John: "For all that is in the world, the lust of the flesh and the lust of the eyes and the pride of life, is not of the Father but is of the world." "The lust of the flesh"; that is sensuality. "The lust of the eyes"; that is outward show. "The pride of life"; that is pretension and humbug with which mortals elevate themselves beyond their merit. Sensuality, outward appearances, pretensions—what words could more adequately characterize the surface quality of secularized living? It is not merely that the pagan lives in this world; it is that his participation in it is so shallow. With skin-deep satisfactions and moment-long interests he roars through life unaware of what he is missing, even imagining that he is living audaciously.

He *is* living dangerously; that we will grant, for his omissions are criminal. He omits to taste the deeper joys of real knowledge, and to acquire the disciplines of genuine skill. In all his getting, he neglects to possess character; and he wastes the treasures of brotherly community in riotous living. That is to say, a human being who is living from the senses and for outward show will compromise and lie; he will ultimately bribe and cheat. His state of mind is the soil of public corruption, of civil strife and of international conflict. Nothing is more surprising to the blithe young pagan than this: to see corruption

growing up in his wake; he did not want to harm anybody; he only wanted to saunter through life without
effort, to enjoy himself, to protect his security and to sur-
vive physical death as long as possible at all costs. He little
understands his moral judgment, and yet its thunder rises
out of the neglected powers of mind and spirit lying deep
within himself—in the God within himself—against
whose holy laws he has offended.

The Christian, however, will do more than perceive
the shallowness and the ultimate evil of pagan living; he
will withstand it and do battle with it. He has orders from
a sovereign above the state; therefore, when the state
commands him to violate his deep sense of the right, his
answer is a creative "No!" In a paganized world, the
positive work of the spirit often begins with a courageous
negative, such a courageous negative as Bishop Otto
Dibelius recommended to the Evangelical Church in
Eastern Germany in his 1949 Pentecostal letter: "We ask
everyone in whose breast a conscience is awake, not to
yield himself to anything that breathes the spirit of vio-
lence and dishonesty. A courageous 'No' to that which
is against the commandment of God, makes one free, even
if the consequence brings danger and distress." In Eastern
Europe and in communized China the evidence grows to
show that the courage which enables a man to say "No"
to triumphant paganism plunges him at once beneath the

surface of life into the depths of soul and spirit. The lust of the flesh, and the lust of the eyes, and the pride of life pass away, giving place to life out of the depths of being, marked on every side by intimations of eternity.

Standing outside the paganism of pagan society, the Christian as alien and exile has eyes to see and heart to withstand the imperfection and evils of the secular order. More than this: he understands the mortal nature of all human societies, and so rises above idolatry.

The temptations of social idolatry are greatly upon us these days. We like to think that we have arrived at ultimate arrangements of things which are perfect incarnations of the will of God for man on earth. What better economic order could be imagined than twentieth-century capitalism, which we delight to label "free enterprise"? What nobler nation could history ever have disclosed than America? And what civilization could ever outstrip Western civilization as we know it? To these economic, national and cultural idolatries on our side of the world, the other half of mankind is today opposing another set of idolatries: communism, Russian nationalism and an entirely different set of cultural values. Each is upheld by its adherents as final and all-embracing truth in the realm of social relations. And these idolatries threaten to destroy one another.

Very subtly and without our awareness of it, the worship of civilization has insinuated itself into our minds. We make the propagation and perpetuation of Western Christian civilization an end in itself and everything else we treat as a means to that end. Even religion is espoused because it seems to be a strong guarantee against cultural decline; thus religion becomes a means toward the end of preserving our civilization. And we are not too clear, either, about what we mean by civilization. We might mean social equality and free inquiry based upon genuine faith in persons and in the power of truth, but more than likely we do not mean these articles of faith and this way of life which lie at the heart of our civilization. We mean something peripheral: automobiles, television and Coca Colas; we mean our standard of living; we mean our comfort and convenience, and we think it very impolite of outsiders to want to disturb us in these enjoyments. After all, we have always thrown them the crumbs from our table.

This is a good time for a man to be able to recognize an idol when he sees one. Our nation and our civilization have become idols to millions of us. It is also a good time for the Christian to remember that the earthly societies of man, like man himself, are mortal. "And the world passes away, and the lust of it, but he who does the will of God abides for ever." The Christian, acknowledging a transcendent citizenship, escapes the idolatry of civilization. He knows with Tennyson that

> Our little systems have their day;
> They have their day and cease to be;
> They are but broken lights of thee,
> And thou, O Lord, art more than they.

Living in a commonwealth with roots in eternity and without boundaries, the Christian is not distressed by the realization that in all probability the United States of America will one day join Egypt and Babylon, Persia and Rome in the dust of history. He loves America, loves her as he loves no nation on earth—it is but human to do so—but he loves the Kingdom of God more. Furthermore, he knows that whatever life America has, she has derived from her partial actualization of the Kingdom of God for a season. As her life becomes progressively superficial, her mortality grows increasingly evident. Multiplying externals and neglecting internal sources, she grows hollow at the center of faith and spirit, and prepares to go the way of all the earth. The Christian will not think of the death of any nation as fated or inevitable. He will work as energetically as any to recreate it from inner, living sources. At the same time, he will know that the last best hope of earth lies, not with any nation, but with God and with the immortal souls of men.

Turn now to a surprising fact: As aliens and exiles,

Christians can be the creators of new temporal societies. It is the judgment of Arnold Toynbee that civilizations are the work of outsiders—he calls them "the internal proletariat." These citizens of a decaying culture, who are in but not wholly of it, by the power of an insurgent faith have many times in history laid the foundations of a new cultural order.

When we approach this matter of social progress we come upon a curious dialectic. For half a century now we have been working consciously and somewhat feverishly at progress. We have had startling results in the realm of technical knowledge and applied science—and we have plunged the world into its greatest wars in history; we have seen the resurgence and augmentation of barbaric cruelties; and we feel ourselves to be living on the threshold of cultural dissolution, which will bring the whole self-confident expedition to a ruinous ending. What can the matter be? There begins to dawn within us the suspicion that the Kingdom of God on earth cannot be *manufactured*; it cannot be directly aimed at and produced by blueprint. It may grow, perchance, when we have given ourselves to those elements of the spirit which look as unlike temporal progress as a grain of corn looks unlike the hardy plant that springs out of the earth where the corn was planted. As the farmer must leave something to sun and rain and the mysterious process of nature, so the creator of cultures plants the seed of his faith and leaves the increase with God.

Think, for example, of the social consequences of John Wesley's campaigns for the souls of men. He aimed directly at no change in the social order. One will search his writings in vain for a sermon on any aspect of the "Social Gospel." Nevertheless, he did change the history of a very great section of English-speaking peoples on both sides of the Atlantic. According to Gerald Heard, the English political scientist and historian, Harold Laski, privately admitted to him "with a sad shake of his head '[Wesley] prevented single-handed the French Revolution coming to England!' One man, an Oxford scholar. He went down and out into the uneducated world to save souls. He cared for men's, individual men's, eternal salvation. And as a by-product, he saved his society, including many who hated him and were indulgent, greedy sinners, from revolutionary destruction."[2]

It is time, perhaps, that we should readmit the other world to the consideration of this one. When the heads of nations feel themselves to be dealing with immortal human souls, they are bound to move in directions calculated to enhance human dignity; but when they regard men as animals, they may use their bodies as stepping-stones toward some imagined future utopia. Indeed, this

[2] Gerald Heard, *Ten Questions on Prayer* (Pendle Hill, 1951), p. 12.

is exactly what all current totalitarianisms are doing; and it is significant that they have to deny all transcendent reality—God and immortality—before they can launch their programs. Triumphant secularism is always *aiming* at the good society for some imagined future, passing through some present hell to get there. Individuals, so long as they are thought of in material terms, may be regarded as steppingstones, as bridges, to the unfulfilled; and so they may be used and discarded as expendables. But persons, who are immortal souls from the living God, may not be so lightly discarded. Thus from a religious perspective a measure of the Kingdom is assured for the present, and a good life on this earth is made possible by the urgent pressure upon it of a real and eternal over-world. Progress for all men becomes possible because the unending growth and development of one immortal human soul is a divine imperative.

Not only does belief in immortality check destructive means for achieving noble ends; it supplies the morale of creative citizenship. Philosopher W. E. Hocking points up this truth for us in a recent essay:

> . . . in order to fight well as a man, one must fight as if one could reasonably disregard danger and even death; and to do this one must believe that there are things in the world more valuable and more enduring than human life itself.

To put the idea into a nutshell: It is impossible, I maintain, to make a reasonable contrast between being a good citizen of this world and having a concern for immortality, because in order to be a good citizen of this world, whether to do a good job or to fight a good fight here, one must have an outlook beyond this world.[3]

We are saying that life is possible in its fullness only to those who have risen above the fear of death. Valuing human life on purely physical terms results in the prostration of degraded human personality before the awful dragon of death. That is the plight of our Western civilization now. From Christian sources, we have learned to think of a human individual as precious. But if the perishable life of the individual is all we have in mind, death, the ultimate evil, will reduce us to cowardly compromises and imprison us within the perishable world of sense and show. Jacques Maritain gives keen expression to this insight, as he points out three possible attitudes toward human life and death:

A civilization which despises death because it despises the human person and the value of human life . . . is not a civilization, but barbarism. [Totalitarianism]

But, on the other hand, a civilization which knows the price of human life but which sets up as its main value the perishable life of man, pleasure, money, selfishness, the possession of acquired commodities, and which therefore fears death as the supreme evil and avoids any risk of self-sacrifice and trembles thinking of death, under the pretext of respecting human life—

---

[3] W. E. Hocking, "Immortality in Science and Philosophy," in *Man's Destiny in Eternity* (Boston, 1949), p. 142.

such a civilization is not a civilization, but a degeneration. Its humanism is cowardly delicacy. [The Modern West?]

True civilization knows the price of human life but makes the imperishable life of man its transcendent, supreme value. It does not fear death, it confronts death, it accepts risk, it requires self-sacrifice—but for aims that are worthy of human life, for justice, for truth, for brotherly love.[4]

We need now to get the dimension of immortality back into our living. Christians, when they are true to their tradition, have this dimension. As aliens and exiles they are not trapped by time, but live free in eternity—and in time. They rise above and stand against the false values of a pagan society. They confront the dissolution of nations and civilizations without the loss of hope. In fact, while intending something far more personal, they become the creative source out of which nations and civilizations rise. And they do all of this as immortal souls, among kindred souls, in the presence of an Eternal God of Truth and Love.

[4] Jacques Maritain, "The Immortality of Man," in *ibid.*, pp. 40 f.

Epilogue: Christians

So Barnabas went to Tarsus to look for Saul; and when he had found him, he brought him to Antioch. For a whole year they met with the church, and taught a large company of people; and in Antioch the disciples were for the first time called Christians. . . . ACTS 11:25, 26

And Agrippa said to Paul, "In a short time you think to make me a Christian!" And Paul said, "Whether short or long, I would to God that not only you but also all who hear me this day might become such as I am—except for these chains. . . ."

ACTS 26:28, 29

If you are reproached for the name of Christ, you are blessed, because the spirit of glory and of God rests upon you. But let none of you suffer as a murderer, or a thief, or a wrongdoer, or a mischief-maker; yet if one suffers as a Christian, let him not be ashamed, but under that name let him glorify God. . . .

I PETER 4:14-16

AT LAST the new faith stumbled upon the one name which came to include all the others and to supersede them; "the disciples were . . . called Christians. . . ." The members of the new fellowship did not invent this name;

it was conferred upon them. They did not welcome it at
first; it was given in derision. In the entire New Testament the new name occurs only three times,[1] and even
then it is found on the lips of outsiders. Thus it seems
that the believers resisted it for many decades, until at last
they must have come to see it in the light of the cross—in-
tended as a mark of shame but to be worn as a badge of
glory.

The name was an invention of the pagan populace of
Antioch, a city which, together with Alexandria, was
famous for its biting witticisms and its derisive nicknames.
When the new faith came to this Syrian city it spilled
over its former Judaistic bounds; no longer restricted to
Jews and Jewish proselytes—so that it could be classified
as a sect of Judaism—the group now expanded to include
gentiles. It became an international and an intercultural
fellowship. Hence it was inaccurate to refer to its adherents as "Jews"; neither was it correct to use old pagan
categories. Here was a society, triumphantly aggressive
and growing phenomenally, which was different from
anything then upon the cultural scene. As outsiders listened to its preaching they caught one word, repeated
more often than the rest, a kind of key word, *Christos*
(Christ). And then some wag who considered himself
"the life of the party," in some Antiochian dining room

[1] Acts 11:26, 26:28, I Pet. 4:16.

or market place, suddenly noticed how like *Christos* was another and a very common Greek word, the word *chrestos*. *"Christos-chrestos-Christos-chrestos."* We hear him chanting it. He had touched off derisive word play so delightful to sophisticated pagan ears. *Chrestos* meant *worthy fellow.* And the followers of this worthy fellow, Christ, were *Chrestians, worthy fellows* themselves! *Christians*—partisans of Christ; *Chrestians*—worthy fellows. The nickname was invented to be spoken sarcastically, much as some sophisticated groups now refer to social uplift workers as "Do-Gooders." In some such manner it must have come about that "in Antioch the disciples were for the first time called Christians."

There is documentary evidence supporting the probability that the first form of the name *Christian* was *Chrestian.* The Codex Aleph, one of the most venerable of New Testament manuscripts, uses it in all scriptural passages where the name occurs. The historian, Suetonius, who reported the banishing of Jews from Rome by the Emperor Claudius in A.D. 49—a banishment in which Aquila and Priscilla were involved (Acts 18:2)—tells us that the Emperor's edict had been issued because "the Jews [of Rome] were in a state of constant tumult at the instigation of one Chrestus." Evidently the Antiochian nickname had traveled to the Imperial City on winged feet; for, Paul and Barnabas labored for a year in Antioch in all probability about A.D. 42 or 43; the Claudian banishment was only six or seven years later.

Even though it was given in derision, the conferring of the nickname was a tribute to the faith of the brethren. It was a tribute to the *vigor* of that faith; outsiders were compelled to take notice of it and to reckon with it. Like many superficial minds who find themselves profoundly disturbed by some new challenge, these outsiders sought at first to dismiss it with a jest, but they were unable to ignore it.

The nickname was a tribute to the *newness* of the Christian faith. Old labels proved inadequate to describe a fellowship in which the accepted barrier between Jew and gentile was dissolved. Imagine a fellowship today vital enough to make a spider web of the iron curtain! It would occasion little more amazement than this new fellowship of Jews and gentiles under the spell of the name of Christ. This newness was cosmopolitan—a barrier surmounting universalism. This universalism was unwittingly captured in the name itself. The word *Christians* was Greek, but it depended upon the Hebrew idea of the Messiah (of which *Christ* is a translation); and the ending of the name was Latin. The name was like the inscription on the cross "written in Hebrew, in Latin, and in Greek." Every man could read its meaning in his own tongue. Here was a faith for all peoples.

The Antiochian tag was also a tribute to the *challenge* of the new faith. The pagan populace found their paganism threatened by it. They felt compelled to attack it by one of the most effective devices known to social control—ridicule. They sought to heap shame upon it. From such raillery it was not very far to the open libels which came to be circulated against Christians in the next century, when they were accused of being atheists, cannibals and sexual degenerates. People do not take the trouble to abuse a movement which they do not fear. Christianity moved into the ancient world as a disturbing, revolutionary force.

Moreover, the name was a tribute to the *nature* of the Christian faith; it was an attachment to a person, not the sponsoring of a system or a dogma. And that person was not simply a man, Jesus of Nazareth. He was Jesus, the Christ—"King of Kings and Lord of Lords," ruling in their hearts at the bidding of God himself. He was not simply a noble man who had suffered martyrdom; he was Truth, and Life and Way. The Antiochians meant to voice no such tribute. They had supposed that *Christ* was a proper name. Therefore, their nickname is all the more revealing in that it is no pun upon the name *Jesus*, but rather upon his cosmic title. The faithful kept trust not merely with Jesus, but with God's anointed. Not only did they follow a teacher; they served their Lord.

It is this conviction of the Personal Truth of God that must take possession of us now. Confronted as we are by a fanatical communist faith in which ardent young men embrace a lie as though it were truth, we cannot long stand embracing Truth as though it were a pleasant fiction. We must embrace that Truth as though it were our very Life and our only Way, believing that the whole universe is for it and against its opposite. To prove that we have such a faith will require something more than a verbal affirmation and a few buildings and symbols bearing that ancient and honorable name. Let Paul say it for us: "For although there may be so-called gods in heaven or on earth—as indeed there are many 'gods' and many 'lords'—yet for us there is one God, the Father, from whom are all things and for whom we exist, and one Lord, Jesus Christ, through whom are all things and through whom we exist." "God has highly exalted him and bestowed on him the name which is above every name, that at the name of Jesus every knee should bow . . . and every tongue confess that Jesus Christ is Lord, to the glory of God the Father."

Set in Linotype Baskerville
Format by Katharine Sitterly
Manufactured by The Haddon Craftsmen, Inc.
Published by HARPER & BROTHERS, *New York*